UNIVERSITY LEADERSHIP AND PUBLIC POLICY
IN THE TWENTY-FIRST CENTURY

A President's Perspective

Canadian universities face a complicated and uncertain future when it comes to funding, governance, and fostering innovation. Their leaders face an equally complicated future, attempting to balance the needs and desires of students, faculty, governments, and the economy. Drawing on more than a decade of service as president of one of Canada's major research universities, Peter MacKinnon offers an insider's perspective on the challenges involved in bringing those constituencies together in the pursuit of excellence.

Clear, contentious, and uncompromising, *University Leadership and Public Policy in the Twenty-First Century* offers a unique and timely analysis of the key policy issues affecting Canada's university sector. Covering topics such as strategic planning, tuition policy, labour relations, and governance, MacKinnon draws on his experience leading the University of Saskatchewan to argue that Canadian universities must embrace competitiveness and change if they are to succeed in the global race for talent.

PETER MACKINNON is President Emeritus of the University of Saskatchewan. From 2003 to 2005 he was the chair of the Association of Universities and Colleges of Canada.

University Leadership and Public Policy in the Twenty-First Century

A President's Perspective

PETER MACKINNON

UNIVERSITY OF TORONTO PRESS
Toronto Buffalo London

© University of Toronto Press 2014
Toronto Buffalo London
www.utppublishing.com
Printed in the U.S.A.

Reprinted 2015

ISBN 978-1-4426-4802-9 (cloth)
ISBN 978-1-4426-1611-0 (paper)

Printed on acid-free, 100% post-consumer recycled paper.

Library and Archives Canada Cataloguing in Publication

MacKinnon, Peter, author
University leadership and public policy in the twenty-first century :
a president's perspective / Peter MacKinnon.

Includes bibliographical references and index.
ISBN 978-1-4426-4802-9 (bound). – ISBN 978-1-4426-1611-0 (pbk.)

1. Universities and colleges – Administration – Canada.
2. Universities and colleges – Government policy – Canada.
3. Leadership – Canada.   I. Title.

LB2341.8.C3M32 2014   378.1'010971   C2014-905160-3

University of Toronto Press acknowledges the financial assistance to its
publishing program of the Canada Council for the Arts and the Ontario Arts
Council, an agency of the Government of Ontario.

University of Toronto Press acknowledges the financial support of the
Government of Canada through the Canada Book Fund for its
publishing activities.

Contents

Preface

It is a feature of aging that memory becomes more prominent in our lives. Among my vivid and most cherished memories are those of visits, as a child, to my grandparents in Montreal and walks with my grandfather from his apartment on University Street to nearby McGill University, where he served as professor of anatomy in the Faculty of Medicine. These walks took us across campus with commentaries by my grandfather on the significance of buildings and other landmarks, and the colourful university personalities associated with them. It is in part to these memories that I attribute a core value of my life: I love universities. I love the big ones and the small ones; the local and distant; the ancient and the modern; the public and private universities. Like all human institutions, they have their peculiarities, vulnerabilities, and weaknesses. But their great strength lies in the fact that it is the merit of an idea that commands respect in a university – not a voice of command, a pronouncement on morality, or a threat of punishment. In a world that witnesses too many commands, pronouncements, and threats, institutions that value ideas, debate, and reasoned conclusions are beacons that give us confidence that we as human beings have a future and that it can be a bright one.

It is this value that inspired this book. Universities are essential to social health and well-being, and to our capacity to address the great questions of this or any day. They need advocates, champions, and exemplars. They also need critics. Canadians need our universities to be the best they can be. I bring thirty-seven years of experience in one of Canada's universities to the writing of this book, and my purpose will have been served if I have illuminated some features of their present condition and pointed to ways of improving them.

viii Preface

This volume is neither memoir nor local history, though it contains elements of both. I introduce each chapter with a vignette from my experience, and inevitably my perspectives are influenced by my career at the University of Saskatchewan, in ways that I make explicit. But the book is about policy, about the choices we make and that are made for us. While my reflections are influenced by my experience, they are not limited by it. My thirteen years as president were concurrent or overlapped with the leadership of some of the finest university presidents in Canadian history. Many of them were my teachers as well as my colleagues, and I hope that their teaching and my learning are reflected in these pages. I have drawn upon their wisdom in addition to the sources listed in the bibliography and notes.

I am grateful to the University of Saskatchewan for the leave that facilitated the writing of this book. My twenty-three years in administration precluded research leaves for which I was eligible during my career at the university, and to have such a leave at the conclusion of my service as president gave me an opportunity to reflect upon the circumstances of Canadian universities and to share my perspective. I am indebted, as well, to David Naylor for introducing me to the University of Toronto Press, and for opportunities to discuss some of the issues with him. I thank John Yates and Daniel Quinlan, at the Press, who patiently listened to my ideas for the book and made welcome suggestions that helped me develop them further. Mr Quinlan added his advice and editorial skills as the volume took shape. Wayne Herrington guided the editorial and production process. Ian MacKenzie was a meticulous copy editor. I am grateful to them and to the anonymous peer reviewers for suggestions that improved the book. Of course, I offer the usual disclaimer that neither they nor the names that follow bear responsibility for its shortcomings; these are mine alone.

My appreciation extends to the Public Policy Forum – to its president, David Mitchell, and to Project Lead Ryan Conway. Mr Mitchell's unfailing enthusiasm and support and Mr Conway's research assistance made the work easier and more enjoyable. Others at the Forum listened to my ideas in group discussions and offered comments and advice. I was pleased to write the book during my two years as the Forum's inaugural Prime Ministers of Canada Fellow – an appointment for which I shall always be appreciative.

William MacKinnon assisted me with research and ideas for chapter 5 and reminded me as only a son can remind a father that, for the book to be of interest to anyone other than me, it must be a work of policy and not a memoir. Susan Bertolo was my assistant throughout my presidency, and her support continued afterwards in the preparation of the manuscript. Herb O'Heron of the Association of Universities and Colleges of Canada (AUCC) gave me tutorials on tuition and financial assistance to students. Michael Atkinson educated me in the ways of path dependency and commented on parts of the manuscript. I thank the four of them warmly.

In addition I am indebted to many people who either read parts of the manuscript, provided information, or made themselves available for discussions or to answer questions: Pat Atkinson, Cheryl Avery, Jim Balsillie, Ernie Barber, David Barnard, Gordon Barnhart, Max Blouw, Wayne Brownlee, Tamara Buckwold, Karen Chad, Barb Daigle, Paul Davidson, Brett Fairbairn, Richard Florizone, Chad Gaffield, Bob Hawkins, Michael Hayden, Agnes Herzberg, Thomas Homer-Dixon, Nancy Hopkins, George Ivany, Laura Kennedy, John Knubley, Alanna Koch, Paul Ledwell, Beryl Lepage, Heather Magotiaux, Rohinton Medhora, Pauline Melis, Jim Miller, Heather Munroe-Blum, Rob Norris, Lea Pennock, Martha Piper, Rob Pritchard, Doug Richardson, Allan Rock, Roy Romanow, Glen Schuler, Mamdouh Shoukri, Jeffrey Simpson, Laura Sommervill, Doug Tastad, Christine Tausig-Ford, Bill Thomlinson, Tom Traves, David Turpin, Peter Stoicheff, Kathryn Warden, and Wayne Wouters.

I must acknowledge, too, that three of my chapter titles are inspired by the cinema and television. "Guess Who's Coming to Breakfast" is a derivative of the 1967 movie of similar name. "Yes Minister" is a title of a British television series of the 1980s. "Let's Make a Deal" is the name of a long-standing American television series.

Above all, to my family – none of whom are reticent about sharing their ideas and opinions – I owe deep gratitude for their wise comments and advice, and for their tolerance and encouragement.

UNIVERSITY LEADERSHIP AND PUBLIC POLICY IN THE TWENTY-FIRST CENTURY

A President's Perspective

Introduction

The College of Agriculture and Bioresources at the University of Saskatchewan is more than a building. It is almost a shrine, a testimonial to the importance of agriculture in a province with more than 40 per cent of the arable land of the second-largest country on earth.

The architecture of the building is commensurate with its stature. Glass and signature university grey stone on the outside frame an interior whose main public feature is an atrium that extends from the building's north door to its south, and nearly to its full height of six storeys.

When the university has something to say to the public, often it is said in the atrium. Invited guests, interested spectators, and curious onlookers assemble with the media on the main floor, or around the second-floor balcony. There is room for hundreds, and it was in the hundreds they gathered on 30 October 1998 to hear that I had been appointed the university's eighth president. The chair of the board of governors and of the presidential search committee summarized the search process and made comments about the reasons for the selection. I replied with remarks of gratitude, acknowledging the magnitude of the assignment and promising to commit myself to the tasks ahead. The media asked questions. Expressions of goodwill and good luck were offered, and the gathering dispersed.

I left the atrium with academic vice-president Michael Atkinson. We reflected on the University of Saskatchewan and on its strengths, weaknesses, and opportunities; and I thought about the evolution of the search that had begun ten months earlier. I began to feel the weight on my shoulders of the announcement that had just been made. "Michael," I asked, "what do I do now?"

The question was a light-hearted acknowledgment that there was no turning back in my career plans for the next decade. It was also an admission of incomplete preparation for an office I knew little about in a public policy context that was ambiguous, if not ambivalent. I had been a professor, a dean, and, for a brief time, a vice-president. I had seen presidents come and go and had impressions of their achievements and shortcomings. But I had limited knowledge of what they did and how they went about doing it. A president's office is largely invisible to the academic community that surrounds it.

I served for thirteen years in the office, and I learned some things that are worth sharing. I learned that a president's duties are multilayered and multidimensional, and that they are never ending. I came to understand how precarious the office is in the midst of the demands and expectations of its several communities. I experienced victories and defeats and rued that the former did not feel as good as the latter felt bad. I left the office in my own time, knowing only that I did the job as well as my capacities permitted.

Much of what I learned has a direct bearing on public policy research and formation. One of the challenges facing universities is misalignment between them and governments. Universities need to ask governments, in ways that are detached from funding requests, how they can help with the latter's policy burdens, and they must do so in the confidence that they are well situated to provide that help. In turn, governments must see universities as having the kind of expertise that can be put to useful work in the service of the country, and they must improve and increase ways of doing so. Canada's universities are nearly all public institutions, and while their personnel may be paid from different purses, they are paid from public sources. They should be seen as partners available to provide knowledge that can help governments solve problems.

This is not a new idea. When both governments and universities were smaller, their relationships were often strong, personal, and easily sustained by people who knew one another. But when both are larger by orders of magnitude, new avenues are needed to facilitate each reaching out to the other. Major challenges such as food and water security, clean energy, sustainable public health care, and an aging population should engage the best minds of the academy and government working together. It is the responsibility of both to bring them together.

It is also clear that universities must overcome barriers to achieve and manage change in general. They are path-dependent organizations with a status quo bias and internal organizations and processes that reinforce that bias. Their histories, governance, unions, and bureaucratic ways combine to discourage change, at least in the absence of imminent threats from exogenous influences. But whatever the internal impulses for altering institutional trajectories, there are many external ones in the current environment. The misalignment mentioned above is one. More explicit and intense competitive influences are others. Technology is a third. Universities must and will change, some for the better and some perhaps not.

The first two chapters are a story about change. The story is that of the University of Saskatchewan, one of Canada's fifteen medical-doctoral universities. It is of general interest because it is an account of positioning, differentiation, and planning that, with modifications appropriate to local circumstances, is applicable to other institutions. Also, it is an account of change involving an attempt to alter a path and not simply incremental adjustment.

The six chapters that follow address major public policy issues facing Canadian universities. Chapter 3 analyses tuition issues, comparing and contrasting approaches in different provinces in an attempt to reach beyond the often puerile public conversations on the subject. Chapter 4 focuses on relationships with governments, academic freedom, and collective advocacy, and explores the tension between closer alignment and university autonomy. Chapter 5 profiles philanthropy and in particular university-industry partnerships, with their concomitant fears of corporatization of Canadian universities. Chapter 6 is concerned with labour relations and the encroachment of collective bargaining on governance and collegial management. Chapter 7 explores the role of universities in advancing the country's scientific capacity. Chapter 8 considers the reasons for the unprecedented high numbers of dismissals or pressured exits from presidential offices and reflects on the changing nature of the Canadian university presidency. An afterword reflects upon the readiness of Canada and its universities for the global race for talent.

There are many policy issues encountered by leaders in post-secondary education, and I do not claim to address all of them. I have sought to present the most prominent themes that dominate conversation about the current state and future of our universities.

Chapter One

Guess Who's Coming to Breakfast:
On Positioning and Differentiation

About twenty-five faculty members were present when I arrived at the Faculty Club for breakfast on 20 April 2001. Since the beginning of my presidency twenty-two months earlier, I had hosted "Breakfasts at the Club" on Fridays when I was in town. Anyone could come, and those who did could raise any issues they wanted to discuss. There was no formal agenda and no commitment to follow up on enquiries or concerns. The purpose of the event was conversation.

It was clear at once that my guests were not present by chance. A long-time faculty member and one-time decanal aspirant was their leader, and he summoned their and my attention by tapping a knife on his glass. He spoke at length criticizing the early months of my presidency. He was troubled by the two themes I had emphasized most: the needs for much improved research performance and greater attention to competitiveness. This emphasis, he suggested, ran counter to university history, circumstances, and culture. He and his colleagues felt that I should drop the message.

The meeting was at once troubling and understandable. It was troubling because it was beyond dispute that the university's research performance was lagging relative to its medical-doctoral peers, and that it had not yet awakened to the reality of intense competition in the post-secondary world. It was understandable because it represented a significant cultural attitude at the University of Saskatchewan: We do things our own way. We march to a different drummer. We do not measure our success by comparisons to others.

This breakfast more than a decade ago represented the choice that had to be made at the University of Saskatchewan: a choice between pursuing and adhering to the standards of excellent universities with responsibilities similar to ours across and beyond the country, or persisting in our current behaviours on the road to a more limited future.

The choice is not for a president alone, but leadership is fundamentally about choices, and no leader can avoid them or defer to the choices of others. The alternative paths facing the University of Saskatchewan at the close of the twentieth century were real and obvious. The question was whether the university, and its communities and supporters, could and would face them – and choose.

The task of positioning a university within its environment must be undertaken by every university in the country. Each one must take account of its history, geography, program array, competitive profile and reputation, and government and community expectations. Because the result is borne of an amalgam of considerations, at least some of which are unique to each institution, we can say that there are ninety-seven universities in the country, and that each is different in significant ways from the others.

This is not always understood by the general public and their elected representatives, who may see universities as more or less the same and distinguishable from one another in only modest or peripheral ways. Their experience with high schools or technical institutes may lead them to think of institutions in terms of generic types, and they may not realize that these schools correspond more readily to a typology than do universities.

To say that universities differ from one another is not to deny two basic propositions: all universities have something in common, and some universities have much in common. What they have in common is that they are academic institutions, which means they have a core of studies that are speculative, theoretical, and scholarly, and that their academic employees must have competence and demonstrated achievement in this realm. That some universities have much in common is an acknowledgment that while their differences defy a comprehensive typology, universities can be distinguished according to class, and that membership in that class yields informative comparisons with others in the same class, and useful contrasts with institutions in another class.

An early Canadian example of such a classification is the two-decades-old *Maclean's* survey.[1] Refined and improved over the years, it has survived criticism and institutional boycotts[2] to become an established feature of the Canadian public post-secondary landscape. It classifies and compares institutions according to whether they are primarily undergraduate, comprehensive, or medical-doctoral. While the extent of its influence is debatable, it appears that readers who purchase the rankings issue in high numbers, international students whose sources of information on Canadian universities are limited, and the universities themselves pay attention to the survey. Indeed the institutions that score well in the rankings celebrate and publicize their success; those that score less well muster their apologia or otherwise downplay the results.

If imitation is the most sincere form of flattery, the *Maclean's* survey has been influential beyond the readership of the rankings issue. What is known as the U15 group of universities[3] is largely the *Maclean's* medical-doctoral class with the addition of the University of Waterloo. Another university group (ACCRU)[4] has as a threshold requirement for membership that the university describe itself as comprehensive. And the appellation "primarily undergraduate" is widely accepted in conversations about differences between and among universities.

The *Maclean's* survey and self-organized groupings such as U15 and ACCRU represented a more explicit differentiation of Canadian universities than we had seen in the past. Where once there were insider understandings and outsider impressions, now there were public lists and numbers. And the differentiation would evolve further as some medical-doctoral universities acquired the moniker "big five" when their presidents publicly challenged what they saw as the historical approach to the country's post-secondary education environment. They argued that a one-size-fits-all or levelling instinct needed to be replaced by policies that would recognize demonstrably outstanding Canadian research universities and help propel them into the highest levels of global rankings.[5]

And there are several of these, together with a growing number of aspirations and initiatives to be among the leading ranks. Among the more prominent ranking systems are the Academic Ranking of World Universities (Shanghai),[6] the Higher Education Evaluation and Accrediting Council Ranking,[7] and the QS Ranking,[8] which in 2010 split into two ranking systems: the QS World University Rankings and the World University Rankings. Although there are different weights and measures among the ranking systems, there is common emphasis on research productivity, impact, and excellence as lead comparisons of quality.

Universities pay attention to these rankings, and sometimes countries declare national ambitions to secure higher places for their universities among them. China's Project 211 and C9 League counterpart to America's Ivy League are among the early signs that Asian universities are improving their standings relative to those in America and Europe. In Canada, satisfaction that four of our universities are in the top one hundred of the Shanghai Index is offset by concern that there are not more, and that none place among the top twenty-five.

Concerns about rankings are not limited to relative placements in them. The dictum that not everything that matters can be measured, and not everything that can be measured matters, applies here and summarizes most of these concerns. More subtly, while employment prospects and some learning outcomes can be measured, they are not comprehensive on the benefits of a good education. Philosopher Mark Kingwell expressed this issue in his criticism of President Obama's idea of tying US federal aid to educational institutions to rankings.[9] "When it comes to valuing education," he writes, "no ratings system or outcomes table can actually penetrate the mystery of why learning is good … When I try to isolate the one outcome that captures education's true value … the best single candidate I can think of is not something quantifiable, nor even a particular idea or set of them: a sense of irony."[10]

Bypassing more casual usages of the word *irony*, Kingwell affirms Edward St Aubyn's definition offered through the voice of his character Patrick Melrose in the novel *At Last* (2011): "that deep-down need to mean two things at once, to be in two places at once, not to be there for the catastrophe of a fixed meaning … Irony of this kind is the opposite of ideology, that bastion of catastrophic fixed meanings. As such, it is a virtue of the democratic imagination, an invitation to think differently, opt out, depart from imposed narratives, be a happiness delinquent. And that's what education is for, finally. Ironically, you can pay for the opportunity but you can't put a price on the outcome."[11]

Kingwell's insight is a warning that rankings are an incomplete picture of the university world. An instrumentalist view of higher education may not recognize or accord weight to values that elude demonstration or measurement. Those values – acknowledgment of ambiguity and the capacity to choose rationally from among ambiguities, and Kingwell's sense of irony – endure across time and fashion. The fact that they are not explicitly acknowledged in the new world of rankings must not lead to their oversight or neglect.

Although in Canada education is a provincial responsibility, the nation's research capacity and performance appropriately engages the federal government, which has taken an interest in international benchmarks of university research performance. Federal cash transfers for post-secondary education have declined sharply over the last two decades, in favour of targeted investments in research.[12] Because many of these investments require, assume, or encourage provincial and other support, the provinces too have become more conscious of research performance and issues. The attention of both levels of government is not misplaced. More of our country's research capacity is concentrated in our universities than is the case in other OECD countries.[13] If Canada is to improve its research and innovation performance, its research universities must play a central role. And the evidence suggests that we have some improving to do. Recent reports of the Competition Review Panel,[14] the Conference Board of Canada,[15] the Council of Canadian Academies,[16] the Science, Technology and Innovation Council of Canada,[17] an expert panel reviewing federal support in research and development,[18] and an expert panel on the state of science and technology[19] cumulatively point to a record in productivity, innovation, and research that requires substantial improvement if we are to be among global leaders.

In themselves, classifications, surveys, and rankings signal only relative standing within broadly defined institutional categories. However, they have been catalysts for wider discussions of differentiation across the country, with variable processes and outcomes.[20] Ontario, home to more than one-fifth of the country's universities, has, in general, deferred to them in their evolution, though in that province both government and universities are now preparing for negotiations to further differentiate them. Late in 2013 the province released a policy framework with six components of differentiation: jobs, innovation and economic development; teaching and learning; student population (access and retention); research and graduate education; program offerings; and student mobility (transfer agreements).[21] In Ontario and elsewhere in Canada, there is growing momentum for further differentiation, which can be expected to focus on similar components together with supporting measurements. What remains to be seen is the extent to which outcomes are negotiated (as contemplated in Ontario) or prescribed.

It is in this context that universities have to choose their futures. Universities are better at talking than they are at choosing, and so it is necessary to overcome inertia by calling them to action. Presidents do this by even more talking. By evoking institutional history, the realities of geography, and the quadrants of a strengths, weaknesses, opportunities, and threats (SWOT) analysis, the universities' circumstances are clarified and its choices made apparent. What does this evocation tell us about the University of Saskatchewan at the turn of the millennium?

It is the fate of university presidents to receive intermittent lectures from faculty members suggesting that they are straying from the path charted by their wiser predecessors. Often it is the first president whose name is invoked in aid of these lessons, and for understandable reasons. Founding presidents are original sources in discussions about what their universities were intended to do, and they have a profound impact in shaping their early histories. The current president is expected to be attentive when the words of the first president are quoted, to acknowledge their wisdom, to align himself more conscientiously with their intent, and if necessary to correct his ways.

The first president of the University of Saskatchewan was Walter Murray. A New Brunswicker in the Philosophy Department at Dalhousie University, he moved west in 1908 in the spirit of first premier Walter Scott's words that Saskatchewan is a big place that needed people with big dreams.[22] By any standard, Murray lived up to these words. He was an excellent founding president and his twenty-nine years in office launched the new university on a path to "an honourable place among the best."[23] He had high standards for faculty recruitment, and the faculty lists during and immediately following his tenure included many names that would have been found among the ranks of outstanding scholars in early and mid-twentieth-century Canada.[24]

Murray's words are also the origin of another description of the university. With the University of Wisconsin in mind as the model to which the University of Saskatchewan should aspire, Murray wrote, "There should be ever present the consciousness that this is the University of the people established by the people, and devoted by the people to the advancement of learning and the promotion of happiness and virtue."[25]

These words could have been the inspiration of premier Walter Scott's subsequent description of the university's new College Building as "the home of the people's university."[26] Thus was born a nickname that was used by some, decades later, to claim that the institution was unique in its emphasis on local service. My breakfast guests in 2001 reflected that claim, though as a view of institutional history it was shared more widely.[27]

All public universities proclaim a commitment to service, and as president of a new university that carried the name of a new province, Murray naturally gave voice to its responsibility to help build Saskatchewan. He could not have known that in doing so, he would inspire a concept of the university that ran counter to his dream that it should have an honourable place among the best universities. Many university employees, and others who would invoke "the people's university" nickname in the years to come, did so for defensive or ideological reasons that placed high value on local service and low cost, and low value on competitiveness, quality, and reputation beyond provincial borders.

The contrast between seeking an honourable place among the best and being a people's university underlies the balancing act that inspired the title of the university's official history.[28] But if we think of a balancing act as an attempt to reconcile different sides or to achieve equilibrium between opposites, it becomes apparent that the metaphor is inappropriate in this context. The pursuit of outstanding quality is not to be modified by the duty of service to a particular community. Indeed the better the university, the better its capacity to serve people or place. Quality is not to be drawn down in the interest of service.

The balancing act at the University of Saskatchewan produced an ambiguity of mission. Over the course of its first century, the institution added colleges and schools that made it one of the nation's fifteen medical-doctoral universities. The responsibilities incurred with this status and the benchmarks of success are not matters for local, idiosyncratic judgment. They are well-established and comparative, and by the turn of the millennium, the University of Saskatchewan was struggling among its peers.

Mission ambiguity within the university inevitably was reflected beyond. As the second half of the century passed, it was commonly said to be trying to be all things to all people or stretching itself too thin. It offered one of the broadest ranges of academic programs in the country, but quality was uneven, as was the quantity and impact of research produced by the faculty. The strongest of their rapidly growing numbers continued to reflect the early vision of an honourable place among the best; others were less ambitious for themselves and their university, and their record of scholarship was modest.

Provincial governments of all three political parties – Liberal, New Democratic, and Conservative – were inattentive, if not indifferent to the provincial university. Nowhere was this more evident than in the relationship between it and the University of Regina, which evolved from the Regina campus of the University of Saskatchewan to an independent institution in 1974. The new university had an ancestry that predated its designation as a branch of the U of S,[29] and there was a credible case for its acquisition of separate degree-granting status. In view of the history,[30] it was not surprising that it grew restless with its branch campus status.

The creation of a separate new university in the provincial capital was a natural development. The mistake that was made in 1974 was not, as some asserted, the establishment of the University of Regina. It was the failure to use the development as an opportunity for considered reflection and policy on the role that each of the two universities would play in the province's post-secondary landscape. That this did not happen explains much of what followed between 1974 and the turn of the century and millennium. With the establishment of separate institutions came the new Saskatchewan Universities Commission responsible for coordinating the universities' programming and rationalizing their budgets. Soon after, a survey of university budget systems was undertaken and a report released in June 1976.[31] Members of the commission agreed that a consensus on funding mechanisms was unlikely,[32] and they were proved correct when it took another quarter century to implement a funding mechanism for the two universities that was activity driven and sensitive to costs.

In 1983 the commission was abolished, with the result that the Department of Continuing Education would deal directly with the universities.[33] For the next eighteen years it did so, with the tension and sometimes acrimony that is foreseeable when two universities seek a larger share of limited resources in the absence of a coherent framework for apportioning them.

In 1996 the Saskatchewan government appointed a special representative to work as a facilitator with the two universities,[34] and Harold MacKay was an excellent choice for the assignment. An accomplished lawyer who understood public institutions as well as the business world, he submitted his report within six months.[35] Its most enduring legacy was the launch of a process to conduct a funding review that might result in changes in the apportionment of provincial monies to the two universities.

The review was conducted by Edward DesRosiers and Associates of Toronto. Commissioned in June 1997, the final report released in October 1998[36] followed seven interim reports, the fifth of which contained a framework with discipline weights confirmed by the participants in June 1998. As it became apparent that a mechanism based on the report would substantiate University of Saskatchewan concerns that existing funding arrangements worked to its disadvantage, the Regina-based opposition to implementing the DesRosiers Report began and would continue for the next four years.

Meanwhile I had taken office as president of the University of Saskatchewan, and one of my first tasks was to press the need for a DesRosiers cost-based activity-driven funding mechanism to properly express the differences between the two universities. And this was the key point. The two universities were different: one was medical-doctoral with a broad range of professional programs, and the other was not. The failure to distinguish between them through a systematically developed funding mechanism worked to the disadvantage of the University of Saskatchewan and undermined its capacity to carry on with existing programs. Either the new funding mechanism had to be implemented or the university would face a diminished future.

But the opposition to the mechanism grew. University of Regina administrators announced that they rejected the multipliers and weights in the proposed framework. Regina-based provincial and municipal politicians took their side. So too did the provincial government department – now called Post-Secondary Education – whose officials talked of an alternative made-in-Saskatchewan mechanism. One senior official in the department said that if the two universities could not agree on the proposed new mechanism,[37] the department was prepared to impose its own solution. The warning of the Saskatchewan Universities Commission in 1978 that consensus on a funding mechanism was unlikely had gone unheeded. The situation required the premier's intervention.

The Government-Universities Consultation Committee represented the latest effort to secure collaboration among the University of Regina, the University of Saskatchewan, and the provincial government. The body was chaired by the premier, so it represented an opportunity to engage the able and nationally respected Roy Romanow in discussions of the important issues in the sector. On 28 February 2000 the committee met around the long table in the Saskatoon Cabinet Office. Present were the premier, the minister of post-secondary education, and other officials of government, together with the board chairs and presidents of the two universities. The minister began by stating that there had to be acceptance by all parties of the DesRosiers framework and thus quickly lent his support to the University of Regina president's statement that the U of R rejected the DesRosiers weights. I replied that it was clearly understood that the weights were part of the framework that was confirmed in 1998. As Edward DesRosiers himself had said, "If you are going to throw out the weights, you have to throw out the whole thing and begin again."[38]

All eyes turned to the premier. He restated the government's commitment to DesRosiers and recognized that consensus may be an ideal but not a reality. "Time has run out" he said.[39] If agreement could not be secured by the end of March, there were two alternatives: the government could make the necessary choice or Mr DesRosiers could be brought back into the province with a view to concluding the process by 1 June. The University of Regina president stated that he was not in favour of bringing DesRosiers back and asked that someone from the ministry take over the task. I replied that only DesRosiers could provide clarification of any issues relating to the proposed funding mechanism.

The 28 February meeting did not conclude the DesRosiers process or halt all efforts to blunt its impact. But the decisive signal had been sent by the premier, and Mr DesRosiers returned to the province to complete his final report, followed by the substantial implementation of his funding mechanism, including its discipline weights and multipliers. After the University of Saskatchewan received some compensation for its historical underfunding relative to the University of Regina, both universities could look forward to operating budget adjustments based on activity and costs, variations that on an annual basis could favour either university. But the principle was established, and there was greater recognition of the reality that the province had two very different universities, and that each had different needs in order to thrive.

Revisiting the nature and role of a university involves considerations of its differences from other institutions in the jurisdiction, and for this the funding mechanism was important. The path in Saskatchewan was more difficult than it might have been, because comparisons are more intense when only two institutions are involved. And the process was exacerbated by the unrealistic commitment of the Department of Post-Secondary Education to implement a funding mechanism only if and when both universities were in agreement. The intervention of Premier Romanow was needed to ensure that the agreed-upon process moved forward, though it did not resolve the ambiguity with which the University of Saskatchewan was viewed by his colleagues.

The governing New Democratic Party caucus was divided on the issue of what kind of university it wanted in Saskatoon. A medical-doctoral university costs a lot of money, and for many in the caucus, the cost was an expenditure only and not an investment. Some among the members mused that if the decision was theirs to make all over again, they would have opted for a polytechnic rather than the medical-doctoral institution that had evolved during the province's first century.[40] For most, the issues facing the universities were not all that important and were accorded low priority on the government's agenda. During my presidency, NDP ministers responsible for the universities were not from the ranks of the most influential members of the government and were changed frequently, with the result that they did not become knowledgeable about and committed to strong public policy in the sector.[41]

If ambiguity or ambivalence about the University of Saskatchewan persisted in the ranks of the governing New Democratic Party, the situation in national and municipal corridors of power was different. In Ottawa "a fundamental rethink of public policy toward researchers and what was expected of researchers and universities"[42] was underway. A pronounced shift to excellence based on competition was emerging as the new public policy. The features of this shift, as described by one of its leaders, were "more of a focus on global excellence; a more strategic approach to research priorities by universities; greater competition and differentiation among research institutions; increased commercialization of research into results; and better links between publicly funded research and the private sector."[43]

Structural changes and new programs followed. The Canada Foundation for Innovation was established in 1997, two thousand Canada Research Chairs were created to attract the most outstanding researchers to our universities, support for some of the indirect costs of research was begun, and the Networks of Centres of Excellence program was expanded. The momentum continued through a change from a Liberal to a Conservative government in Ottawa. Under the new government, the Canada Excellence Research Chairs (CERC) – first twenty, then thirty – to bring some of the world's best researchers to Canada were established. The Knowledge Infrastructure Program was geared to maintaining and improving research facilities in universities, and the Vanier and Canada Graduate Scholarships were introduced.

In the municipal context of Saskatoon, the prominence of the university was growing. On a busy day, about 15 per cent of the city's residents studied or were employed on campus. As the city developed, it became apparent that the campus was in the city centre, not out of sight and out of mind across the South Saskatchewan River or in the suburbs. Its impressive grounds underlined what careful observers had known for years: the university was at the centre of the city's cultural, social, and economic life.

Now the city was paying more attention. New theorists were writing about the positive influence of universities on urban development and on the social and cultural sophistication that attracts newcomers.[44] What Richard Florida called the "creative class" was seen as a catalyst for more worldly and attractive cities and a boon to economic development.[45] Saskatoon's Mayor Don Atchison gave strong and frequent voice to the interrelated destinies of city and university.

In summary, this was the context, present or proximate, in which I began my new duties in 1999: despite its promising origins and early history, the University of Saskatchewan did not thrive in the middle to later years of the twentieth century. It experienced substantial growth, with rapid increases in faculty from about two hundred in 1950 to approximately a thousand in 1975. Many of the new recruits were excellent; many were not. The university's productivity did not keep pace with its growth and with its responsibilities as the only medical-doctoral university in the province. Its administrations were preoccupied by the issues of the day and did not publicly assert and defend a vision of the university that had a chance of prevailing against internal division and that element of the university culture that undermined Walter Murray's vision that the university should have an honourable place among the best.

The external provincial environment reflected the ambivalence of mission within. Despite the premier's timely intervention to honour the DesRosiers process and funding mechanism, his government and caucus had significant numbers who were indifferent to the University of Saskatchewan, and some regretted that they had a medical-doctoral institution rather than a polytechnic on their hands.

But there was a change underway in Ottawa and Saskatoon. Canada needed to strengthen its research capacity and graduate education, and new federal government attitudes and initiatives signalled higher ambitions and challenges for the nation's universities. New thinking about cities emphasized universities as principal agents of creativity and economic development, and Saskatoon's leadership expressed its agreement. The stage was set for a new expression of the university's mission and for engaging the city, province, and country on its road ahead.

Public policy, including the positioning of a university in its local and wider environment, entails choices, and choices are always limited. A university president has only one opportunity to fundamentally influence the long-term development and shape of her university. If you get it wrong, you are unlikely to have an opportunity to get it right. Even if you get it right, it takes a long time to produce results. Times in these offices are brief – typically a maximum of ten or twelve years, and often much shorter – and universities are slow to change. If major change is indicated, the process can take years. By the time a message of change is developed, refined, and delivered, and its influence felt and acted upon with identifiable results, a presidential term will be advanced, if not complete.

The first choice to be made was whether ours would remain a medical-doctoral university. Problems in the College of Medicine were coming to a head, and one informed observer predicted that "the college is going to implode."[46] During its first half-century there had been heavy emphasis on the role of the college in the delivery of medical services and insufficient recognition that good medical schools have three robust missions: clinical service, teaching, and research. The latter two occupied distant second and third places in the university and provincial medical communities, and the college was at the bottom of a list of Canadian medical schools in the attraction of Medical Research Council (later CIHR) research funding. Its relations with the Saskatoon Health Region were poor. There was no patient-oriented clinical research space in the city or province. The culture within the college was entrenched and resistant to change, and promising faculty were either avoiding or prematurely leaving the college.

The province's minister of health, Pat Atkinson, and I met to discuss the issues during the summer of 1999. For me the first question was whether the government remained committed to medical education in the province. If the answer was no, I was prepared to consider seeking dissolution of the college, but Minister Atkinson's answer was definitive. The province needed the College of Medicine to attract the personnel to provide general and specialized health-care services. Although the ramifications of her answer would be felt for years to come, this much was now clear: the university would remain a medical-doctoral institution.

That settled, I began to talk frequently and publicly about research performance and competition. I knew that university presidents often think their words are more influential than in fact they are. In general, their audiences listen respectfully and occasionally nod affirmatively; sometimes they may even applaud. It is tempting to conclude that an issue has been identified and framed and that those who are involved will follow up. The reality is that words are soon forgotten as members of the audience return to their daily tasks. It was this reality that moved provost Michael Atkinson to caution that words were not enough. We needed to signal and explain our major strategic emphases and secure their legitimacy within the university and support for them in the wider community.

In response to the provost's advice, I prepared a strategic directions statement and presented it to university faculty and staff, government officials, and members of the board of governors on 24 November 2001.[47] This statement, and the follow-up to it, would be my one chance to profoundly influence the long-term development of the university. It was ultimately approved by the institution's tri-partite governance bodies and remained my guide and touchstone for the nearly eleven years that remained in my term in office. Like all such documents, there were layers of specific goals and objectives, but the three broad strategies were as simple as they were important.

The first was a commitment to the best national and international standards of medical-doctoral universities. There is a sense in which (in colloquial terms) this was a no-brainer, but it was important that we at the University of Saskatchewan make that commitment to ourselves, precisely because we had not always lived up to it, and there was an element of the university's culture that felt it didn't matter. It was important that competitively high standards be official university policy and that practices be adopted to require compliance by all. These practices included tightening the standards for promotion and tenure; implementation of systematic program review and publication of results; and adoption of performance measures that we called an "achievement index" to measure progress through time.

The second strategic direction was the most controversial. It committed the university to identifying areas of existing strength and investing in them so as to establish their pre-eminence. This was my choice of words and it was deliberate. In the course of developing the strategic directions, I was urged on several occasions to substitute *excellence* or other words and combinations of words for *pre-eminence*. I remained adamant, because the alternatives would introduce ambiguity into the exercise. We all know that excellence is fungible and, like beauty, exists in the eye of the beholder. Pre-eminence is not. It means the best in the world or at least one among the best in the world. It establishes the highest standard and can be measured according to criteria that are well understood in the academic world.

The process of identifying areas of existing comparative strength would be important in itself. Quality in the university was uneven, but unevenness was rarely spoken about in public, let alone measured. Zero-sum arguments were common: selective investments would "rob Peter to pay Paul" and create winners and losers. The idea of officially acknowledging unevenness and singling out areas of strength for further investment was untested, if not frowned upon by some. "We're all trying to do our best" was a familiar refrain in support of treating strengths and weaknesses in the same way. It was an unfortunate misapplication of the principle of equality.

Identification of areas of strength for elevation to pre-eminence would accomplish several goals. It would allow us to better define our mission and to explain it to others; it would help attract resources to build on strengths; it would encourage academic units to collaborate in seeking to bring some of their activities within or closer to identified strengths; and it would expose areas of the university that needed to improve. In summary, it would establish excellence as commonly understood and measured in the academic world as the standard at the University of Saskatchewan.

Of course an endeavour such as this had to be credible. Potential pre-eminence cannot be touted if it is so far from reality as to be silly. The areas identified as existing strengths had to be compelling. The process, too, had to be credible. Although I had strong views of what the areas should be, and confidence that any sensible process would identify them, it was not for me to reveal and announce them. Research vice-president Karen Chad led the process to identify six areas that subsequently were approved:

1. Aboriginal Peoples: Engagement and Scholarship
2. Agriculture: Food and Bioproducts for a Sustainable Future
3. Energy and Mineral Resources: Technology and Public Policy for a Sustainable Future
4. One Health: Solutions at the Animal-Human-Environment Interface
5. Synchrotron Sciences: Innovation in Health, Environment, and Advanced Technologies
6. Water Security: Stewardship of the World's Freshwater Resources

For all of these, a combination of existing academic strengths and resources joined with geographic opportunity to make them appropriate areas for efforts to elevate them into the world of pre-eminence. A team of fine historians joined with legal scholars and others to make the U of S already strong in Aboriginal areas. Saskatchewan has the largest percentage of Aboriginal people of any province in Canada and a grow-ing young Aboriginal population. Working with them to ensure their success is one of the great social imperatives of twenty-first-century Canada.

The College of Agriculture and Bioresources, together with the excel-lent Crop Development Centre, were joined by a new $50 million Global Institute for Food Security to create a unique capacity for investigation of food-related issues in one of the country's and world's most impor-tant agricultural regions. Saskatchewan's mineral wealth, a new grad-uate School of the Environment and Sustainability, and a historically strong Department of Geology supported the identification of energy and mineral resources as one of the select areas. The presence of Col-leges of Medicine and Veterinary Medicine, a new International Vaccine Centre, a new Graduate School of Public Health, and one of the univer-sity's two CERC chairs made One Health an irresistible selection. The presence of the country's only light source, a third-generation synchro-tron on the university campus, made synchrotron sciences an obvious choice. And Canada Excellence Research chair Howard Wheater lead-ing a superb team of water and environmental experts made freshwater security another compelling choice.

The third strategic direction was an affirmation of sense of place. The province and university were established only two years apart, the lat-ter as one of the foundational institutions in the young province. Its development was eagerly awaited, and ambitions for it were high.[48] A large land grant anticipated the size and scope of the university, as well as the role it would play in developing the province's agricultural industry. This was Saskatchewan's university, and both province and university were going places.

Presidents are reminded of the ambitions of their university's found-ers in many ways. In my case, one of the reminders was the fine resi-dence at the southwest corner of the campus overlooking downtown across the South Saskatchewan River. All seven of my predecessors lived there, and when I naively resisted doing so before my appointment, I was given to understand that the invitation to serve as president and to occupy the residence was joint: they could be accepted or declined together.[49] Later I came to understand why. The residence's elegance and physical presence made it an ideal setting for university hospitality, and subsequently I would be the host of hundreds of events there. More subtly, this impressive building was a symbol of the high ambitions that the founders had for the new university and would remind presidents in their daily lives that much was expected of them.

However impressive, a campus is only the immediate expression of sense of place. The connections between what happens on campus and the communities that surround it give substance to the definition of place. With any university in any community, these connections are innumerable – professional, cultural, financial, commercial, athletic, social, and personal – and they are ties that bind university and community together. A president is part of these, of course, but she is also expected to give public voice to the scope and meaning of these ties and so to remind university colleagues and community members of their importance.

This articulation of how a university sees itself and relates to its communities is a task primarily for its president. It is shared with others in the university, and the voices may be many and sometimes discordant. The president is seen as speaking for the entire campus and his messages are understood as closer than any others to being official. They are listened to and reported, and they are received with interest, reassurance, or concern, or a mixture of these. Clarity, credibility, and inspiration in delivering these words are important for success of both university and president.

A president speaks publicly so often that he may fear – perhaps realistically – that he is boring his audiences as well as himself to death. But frequent communication is part of binding the ties between community and university. This communication must be extended outward, because universities – some more than others – have provincial, national, and international reach. In Saskatchewan the provincial reach is critical. At the beginning of my term I launched a provincial tour that continued until I left office. This tour took me to smaller cities and towns in the province. Long days on the road typically began with breakfast meetings with high school administrators and guidance counsellors, followed by talks to and with local high school students. Meetings with chambers of commerce, municipal officials, service clubs, nearby Aboriginal communities, health region officials, and alumni followed before an evening reception and late return journey to Saskatoon. Regular visits ensured that the tour was seen as an ongoing conversation rather than a one-stop public relations exercise. It was an important part of asserting that the university's place was Saskatchewan and not only Saskatoon.

There are other spatial dimensions to a university's place. The University of Saskatchewan is a western Canadian, great plains, and northern institution, as well as a provincial one. Each of these dimensions provides opportunities and implies responsibilities for the university. Western Canada has growing influence in the Canadian federation; its post-secondary and research institutions should reflect and contribute to that growth. The Great Plains of North America cover 1.3 million square kilometres in the prairie provinces and parts of ten states, with globally important capacity in food and energy. Universities in the Great Plains region have vital roles in developing that capacity. And with Saskatoon's location as one of the most northerly of mid- to large-size Canadian cities, university connections to a growing north are increasingly important.

Positioning a university within Saskatchewan requires attention to the province's demographic of Aboriginal people. With nearly 15 per cent of a population of 1.1 million, and with a cohort younger than that of non-Aboriginal people, it is clear that future successes of the province and its Aboriginal residents are interdependent. Education, including post-secondary education, is essential to their full participation in the economic, social, and political life of the province.

Shortly after I became president of the U of S, the president of the Regina-based Saskatchewan Indian Federated College, subsequently renamed the First Nations University of Canada, suggested that his institution assume responsibility for the education of Aboriginal university students in Saskatoon. SIFC would mount its academic programs in a building it would construct on U of S land – an approach similar to that at the University of Regina. It might have a federated or other relationship with the U of S, but the core idea was a separate institution specializing in the education of Aboriginal people. I declined this offer, because I thought it risked de facto segregation of Aboriginal students, with the result that they would not be exposed to the broad range of academic programs and opportunities on our campus.

The alternative – one more appropriate to institutions like the University of Saskatchewan – is to adopt policies and practices that will ensure accessibility for Aboriginal students to all university programs and participation by a critical mass of these students in the life of the university. This more integrated model requires institutional commitment and resources on a large scale, and these were made at the University of Saskatchewan. The result is seen today, with more than two thousand Aboriginals (approximately 10 per cent of all students) enrolled in the university's thirteen colleges. The university's chancellor and student union president are Aboriginal, and a new student centre – a signature design by Aboriginal architect Douglas Cardinal – is taking shape in the midst of the traditional collegiate gothic architecture of the campus. It will be a centre where all students can come together in a cultural context that is intended to promote greater understandings among them.

Sense of place in the international context is embedded in the global reach of a university's academic and service activities and the priority accorded to them within the institution. While these vary from one institution to another, many if not all Canadian universities share the burden of our country not being seen as a preferred destination for foreign students. A report commissioned by the federal government and led by Western University president Amit Chakma[50] observes that while Canada should be a top destination for international students, we are behind other western countries in recruiting them. Dr Chakma's task force proposes doubling the number of international students studying in Canada within ten years. To achieve this goal, our universities should recruit under a common Canadian brand, target countries where we have high potential to recruit students,[51] and offer competitive scholarships to attract more of the best of these students. Early in 2014 the Government of Canada announced implementation of the Chakma Report and committed resources to double the number of international students in Canada, and to encourage more Canadians to study abroad.[52]

Any discussion of sense of place in spatial terms must take account of the virtual reality created by new and emerging technologies. Will the internet, Massive Open Online Courses (MOOCs) designed and overseen by the world's greatest scholars, and distance learning fundamentally alter what it means to say, "I am going to university"? If a university can come to us, does it not render obsolete or passé our traditional understanding of physical transference to a campus on which we live or to which we commute? Will large parts of the traditional campus fall into disuse some day, to be seen as monuments to a quaint past, while faculty and administrative offices become high technology call centres by which virtual contact and interaction are facilitated and mediated?

These are serious questions, and our answers to them are incomplete. We know from experience that the impact of new technology is often either exaggerated or underestimated. It changes the way we do things, but it does not change all that we do or who we are. We are social beings, and in general we like to be in the company of one another – not virtual but physical company, where we can sometimes touch one another or take pleasure or comfort from others' presence. And so we will continue to gather together, even though we could do some of what we want to do virtually.

For many, going to university is part of acquiring independence and growing up. For increasing numbers, it is accessing learning opportunities where they live and work. For still others, it is participating in life-long learning for vocational or other practical reasons, or simply for the joy of learning. Large numbers – particularly, though not exclusively, in graduate studies – pursue research requiring special facilities. Considering the many motivations for university education, we can predict that people will continue to go to university for reasons that will draw them to our campuses. Geographic sense of place will not be replaced by virtual sense of place.

But virtual reality and possibilities will increase competition. Weaker universities will be vulnerable. Those that experience more than the usual difficulties in adjusting to change, including change brought by new technology, will fall behind. Some will be diminished. Some will close. But those that sustain already outstanding reputations, or that have their sights firmly on excellence and on the quality of the experience of the many learners that look to them, will flourish. Their campuses will remain places of inspiration and beauty, their sense of place reassured.[53]

Sense of place is not only geographical or spatial. A university gauges itself in part by comparison to others that offer a similar range of programs. In this respect the 2011 invitation to the University of Saskatchewan to join the U15 was an important development in its modern history.

Established in 1991 as the Group of Ten,[54] it expanded in 2006 when Dalhousie and the universities of Calgary and Ottawa were added, and again in 2011 when Manitoba and Saskatchewan joined the group. These are the country's most research-intensive universities, and their common cause is to encourage public policy that recognizes their prominent roles in research and graduate education: 80 per cent of all university research, more than 75 per cent of federal research grants with more than three-quarters of all doctorates awarded in the country.[55] I sought U of S membership in the U15 because I wanted it to be understood locally that our peers were the other universities of this group, and nationally that University of Saskatchewan success is important not only to the province and region, but to Canada. With annual research funding of more than $200 million[56] and two of the country's major science installations,[57] the stakes for U of S success

had risen rapidly. If some of the academic units that lag behind others (principally medicine) improve their research success to at least
the level of U15 averages, the university has every prospect of moving into the top echelon of U15 universities. In doing so, it would at
last achieve the ambition of its first president to secure an honourable
place among the best universities.

Chapter Two

What's the Plan?: On the Pursuit of Goals

Blaine Holmlund was University of Saskatchewan vice-president (planning) when he arrived at my office in the College of Law one afternoon in 1986. I knew the vice-president only slightly and did not anticipate the reason for his visit, but he came quickly to the point. He asked me to join his planning group working on issues and options for the university's future. I reminded him that I was a law professor and knew nothing about planning. This admission of ignorance did not deter him, or me for that matter, and I agreed to a part-time secondment to his office.

In my early experience, the idea of a university plan seemed to be either hallucinatory or an oxymoron. Most administrators appeared to be preoccupied with operations and to have little time or inclination for imagining the institutional future, let alone attempting to construct or even to frame it. These were the latter years of establishing new universities and growing existing ones to accommodate the baby boomers, and the attention of university administrations was understandably directed to expansion. Many faculty were too focused on their scholarly and other activities to be interested in any but a prosaic way in what lay ahead for their university. Some of them were suspicious of motivations for planning, and fearful it reflected the administration's determination to have its own way. Then there is serendipity. The idea that planning is antithetical to the fortuitous accidents and unforeseen successes of scholarly investigation is common in the academy. "Let a thousand flowers bloom" is an injunction with origins in mid-twentieth-century China[1] but it also expressed a value, respected in the academy, that talented people working freely will do unplanned, creative, and occasionally great things.

Juxtaposed with this experience is the reality that planning (whether casually or more systematically) is pervasive in our public and private lives. We hear of tax plans, succession plans, estate plans, game plans, and family plans. Businesses and governments plan. People plan for the summer and for the weekend. Whether in our occupational or personal lives and whether we plan well or badly, we see ourselves as planners.

External influences brought pressure on universities to take a more orderly approach to their internal affairs. If previously governments had been tolerant of non-existent or weak plans, they no longer were.[2] More prominent and explicit competition, local and global, required organized responses. Philanthropists and other investors and supporters expected requests for financial support to rest on a clear sense of direction and priorities. "What's the plan?" was becoming a more pressing question for universities, as for other organizations.

There are two antecedent questions, the answers to which cannot be assumed or ignored: why plan? and what is planning? In addition to a need to respond to external influences that act on all organizations, writers say we plan in order to be rational about the future, to assert what control we can over it and to formulate strategy[3] – in other words, to plan. The tautology may be the origin of the idea that the process of planning is an end in itself, that it is a way of making decisions that is at least presumptively better than its more impulsive rivals. But even if planning as process is continuous, actual plans – however contingent – must crystallize along the way. We do not plan for its own sake but to make a plan.

In answering the second antecedent question, Henry Mintzberg considers five definitions by which planning is variously said to be future thinking, controlling the future, decision-making, integrated decision-making, or a formalized procedure to produce an explicit and integrated system of decisions.[4] The extent to which planning is – or is more than – managing, creating, or deciding is a subject that itself has attracted some attention, though it is the ideas of integration and formalization that give robust meaning to the concept. Integration is a process of interrelating the elements of a decision or, more importantly, different decisions. But because integration may be intuitive, episodic, or even haphazard, "something more is needed to identify planning,"[5] and that something is formalization or systemization of the process.

The enterprise carries a high risk of failure. In 2000 Korschgen, Fuller, and Lambert[6] observed that some colleges and universities had "profited immeasurably" from their strategic planning efforts, while others

institutions to refuse "to appropriate the procedures of modern management."[15] But that was beginning to change, he said, because of more
intense external pressures on universities and colleges, together with
the influence of a new convergence between business and government
in the field of planning.[16] Universities were beginning to join other
large organizations in recognizing a need for strategic planning, not
as an imitator of them, but according to their own circumstances and
potentials.

Keller's work remains influential today because of his timeless
reminders of what strategic planning is and is not. Strategic planning,
he said, "involves continuous adjustments to shifting conditions, with
a central strategy in mind."[17] It is not a blueprint, a set of platitudes, an
exclusive vision of president or governors, an aggregation of academic
and administrative unit plans, an abandonment of history, or the product of an annual retreat. It is a determination to shape the university's
future rather than have it shaped by external conditions. It is a commitment to strong management, to being participatory, to responding
to the external environment, to being competitive, to concentrating on
making decisions, and to the future of the university above all else.[18]

In addition to its recent history the University of Saskatchewan faced
formidable barriers to engaging in strategic planning to lift its horizons
and improve its prospects. Its academic governance shortcomings persisted into the century's last decade, and any attempt to change them
was resisted by a politically connected faculty union that recognized
governance weaknesses as one of the most important sources of its
own influence.[19] But now there was a president determined to address
the issue. George Ivany had the benefit of experience at universities in
Canada and the United States when in 1989 he joined the U of S as
its seventh president and immediately recognized the sorry state of
its governance as one of the greatest problems confronting the institution. Acting on one of the few reports to emerge from the Issues and
Options exercise,[20] he fielded his own team of allies to counter faculty
union lobbyists and persuaded the provincial government to introduce
new legislation creating a representative council with strong academic
authority.[21]

The university and provincial government had now removed the
principal institutional barrier to strategic planning. Within a few years
the university appointed Michael Atkinson as vice-president academic
and soon to be its first provost. He was to become the planning champion the institution needed, as well as the principal architect of the

process. The hurdles in his way were formidable and the stakes were high. If the University of Saskatchewan could not change, it would continue on a path to become a weaker, diminished institution. Successful planning could alter its path, lift its horizons, and inspire its enthusiasts and supporters. But would it work?

The provost introduced the concept of integrated planning in 2001. It was not an abrupt turn from an environment in which no planning was contemplated. The work of vice-president Holmlund had raised the need to plan in the consciousness of the community. The new university council had cut its teeth by producing a new planning document.[22] The provost had led a priority determination process that, though modest in scale, was a competitive process of the kind that was seen by many to be against the grain of the University of Saskatchewan. "These were ways of getting something moving. Each step was a rehearsal for what was to come. They gave us the courage to go bigger."[23]

The process that was launched in 2001 was intended to integrate existing and new planning initiatives as well as to produce a product, an integrated plan. A statement of guiding principles promised a process that would be open, comprehensive, structured, powerful, consultative, action-oriented, streamlined, flexible, and accountable. The most visible early product was the strategic directions statement described in chapter 1. It was essential that, as the first prominent initiative of integrated planning, the statement reflect the guiding principles. It was months in the making and involved consultations and workshops that attracted the participation of hundreds of people from the university and wider communities. Governing bodies were briefed regularly on its development and approved it as a document outlining the university's distinguishing features and strategic priorities, and the environment needed to foster them.

The necessary companion to the strategic directions statement was a description of the main elements of the process. These were outlined by provost Atkinson in an address to the university community in early 2002, which was then discussed in various forums before its publication in the fall of that year. The Provost's White Paper on Integrated Planning emphasized the importance of integration on several levels: planning and budgeting, financial oversight, academic and administrative planning, inclusion of semi-autonomous units, and a more deliberate approach to evaluation. Integration to this extent could be achieved only within a realistic time horizon, one that was multi-year rather than immediate or short term. "One-year budgeting and year-by-year hiring is not conducive to a consideration of how units can best achieve their diverse missions. In a one-year framework the focus is on the immediate and on the individual. The interests of the unit as a whole, let alone the university, are seldom given the attention they deserve."[24] Multi-year budgeting would be an essential element of integrated planning. Certainly there needed to be provision for fluctuations in revenue sources and unanticipated events, but a five-year time frame would allow for planning, as opposed to exigent and reactive management.

The provost also described a new decision-making structure to undertake the burden of integrated planning. The main integrative and budget advisory body would be known as the Provost's Committee on Integrated Planning and would be responsible for planning parameters and multi-year budget recommendations to the board of governors based on a review of the plans of all academic and administrative units. This would be supported by an administrative committee responsible for advice on the resource plans required to support strategic initiatives, and by an integrated planning office responsible for institutional analysis and budget planning.

As the provost pointed out, a decision-making structure like this might inspire university people to ask, "Whatever happened to the good old days when you could call up one vice-president or another or form a delegation and march to the President's Office?"[25] The answer, of course, is that there was a new urgency to substitute collegial decision-making for the one-off consideration that often flowed from opportunism and influence. Integrated decision-making would be required of the entire university, including its most senior administrators. Decisions to spend money or to invite the board to spend money would not be made by the president's executive at Monday morning meetings. They would be made within the discipline of the integrated planning process.

To give substance to the process, a series of foundational documents was proposed and developed. In addition to the planning documents themselves, the most pressing initiative involved new standards for tenure and promotion. Faculty and administrators at the University of Saskatchewan were familiar with comments in external letters assessing eligibility for tenure or promotion that said in effect that the candidate would not meet the standard at the referee's university but might meet the standards at the University of Saskatchewan. Such a discrepancy in standards should never have been permitted to develop but with an anticipated generational turnover of faculty by the hundreds, it had to be ended.

The development of new standards for promotion and tenure is not what one would expect to be a planning initiative. It had become one because the new provost had inherited a languishing initiative on standards from his predecessor. It had previously been seen as an editing task, but it quickly became apparent that the problem was the standards themselves. "The core of the problem was in the research expectations."[26] They were not serious standards for a university with research ambitions. College standards were variable – high in engineering, low in medicine – and a short waiting period for tenure was seen by some not as a standards problem but as a recruitment tool.

The proposed new standards were resisted by the faculty union and others. The objection originated in the idea that change, if there was to be any, had to be bottom up. It had to come from the grass roots, from individual units and not be imposed from the top. However compelling and pressing the need for change, the task of university-wide bodies was to wait until the will to act differently percolated in departments and colleges and made its way into the councils of the university. It might do so; it might never do so. But that was the way things had to be done.

It took patience for the university review committee chaired by the provost to prevail. They consulted with all college tenure and promotion committees, in some cases beneficially, "and produced a set of standards that seriously required performance."[27] But the process and result were important for more than this reason. Though its inclusion within integrated planning was accidental, this first initiative was successful and encouraged the belief that more was possible, and there was much more to come.

The new standards were the first of a series of university statements on a host of critical areas. These foundational documents were to be university-wide planning documents signalling the direction the university should take within the framework of the Strategic Directions. They included an enrolment plan, a plan for research, scholarly and artistic work, and plans for Aboriginal initiatives, internationalization, faculty complement, information and communications technology, the campus core area, and administrative units. These documents, together with plans from the thirteen colleges and the results of a systematic review of all university programs, would be the base for the preparation of the university's first integrated plan.[28]

The first four-year plan was followed by a second[29] and a third.[30] For over a decade, integrated planning has been a reality at the University of Saskatchewan, and two questions present themselves: has it made a difference, and has it made a difference sufficient in scale to disrupt the institution's path dependency? The answer to the first question calls for a comparison between where the institution was before integrated planning began, and where it was a decade later. "Our situation is one of incredible stress,"[31] said the provost in 1999 before the advent of integrated planning. The university's budget had been stagnant for some years and when adjusted for inflation was four-fifths of what it had been at the beginning of the 1990s. The university had lost 123 faculty members while student numbers had grown. "We began the journey of integrated planning in an environment where decisions were experienced as 'a series of one-offs, responsive to opportunities or threats, but in no way actually asserting a coherent agenda. The community was full of suspicions ... Cutbacks had lowered trust in one another and raised anxieties that no priorities would emerge and that everyone would be diminished. The planning horizon was one year at best.'[32] The university had no statements on matters of fundamental academic and strategic importance such as enrolment, Aboriginal initiatives or research."[33]

The issues that needed to be addressed if the university were to up its game were many: too few graduate students and declining numbers of them; subpar research funding, particularly in tri-council support; rigidity in workload assignments to the detriment of research and administrative work; lack of systematic program review; overdue programmatic and curricular review; and a need for major investments in capital, particularly for research space and for residences where there had been no building since the 1970s.

The accumulation of issues was such that the goal could not be simply to improve on this or that issue. Integrated planning would be about "creating a different kind of university."[34] As the process developed, the expectations for it were refined. The rigid and confining organizational structure needed to be challenged to create new structures and programs; priorities would be identified; evidence-based decision-making would be the norm; difficult decisions would be made about disinvestment and investment; and higher standards in administration and management would be required.

What actually happened? The operating budget more than doubled between 2001 and 2012,[35] allowing new and substantial investments in the university's programs and activities. An academic priorities fund became an important source of strategic spending. Major

investments were made in university advancement; three new inter-
disciplinary graduate schools were created; investment in student
awards saw the number of students receiving them triple; compensation was made more competitive; distributive and professional education were expanded; and substantial investment was committed to
experiential learning. There was a 74 per cent increase in the number
of graduate students.

Research and infrastructure witnessed substantial transformation.
Growing financial support for research enabled the university to claim
twelfth place among the ninety-seven Canadian universities in total
research revenue. Investment in infrastructure between 1999 and 2012
exceeded $1.2 billion for scores of major and minor projects, including
two of the largest science investments in modern Canadian history.[36]
Two of thirty Canada Excellence Research Chairs were awarded to the
university in highly competitive processes.

Was there change on a scale to alter the university's path or trajectory?
The literature on the subject of path dependency[37] highlights the use of
the term in both a broad and a narrow sense. The broad sense – history
matters – is self-evident and has limited explanatory power because of its
generality, but it does convey an important idea: "[A] dynamic process
whose evolution is governed by its own history is path dependent."[38]
An unfolding historical narrative, whether of institutions or social phe-
nomena, is influenced in substantial and persistent ways by each step
or event in the narrative. Cumulatively these steps or events reinforce
a historical trajectory and make departure from it less likely and more
difficult. A current path may not be inevitable but it is the path of least
resistance, and in that sense it has momentum.

In the present context, this means that integrated planning to create –
in the provost's words – "a different kind of university" is change
aimed at disrupting path dependency and its self-reinforcing ways. It
is this quality of self-reinforcement that makes the task a formidable
one. An established path that pays scant attention to competitive influences and external criteria for evaluation is an easier path, easier for
faculty and administration and less expensive for government, and
they become its committed if not its fully conscious stakeholders. It is
for this reason that path dependency has been likened to sleepwalking
through history.

We can be more confident about judging incremental changes and
their cumulative significance than we can be about determining whether
a new path has been substituted for an old one. History may not repeat

itself, but its impact is recurring. An old way of doing things does not easily give way, and even where it does, it may come back. Despite the optimism that comes with generational change in academic personnel, we must be cautious in our judgment whether the era of integrated planning at the University of Saskatchewan marks a new path, or incremental improvements along an old one. In this, as in so many things, time will tell.

Chapter Three

White Coats Make an Office Call:
On Tuition and Financial Assistance
for Students

I had advance notice of a visit from medical students unhappy with a tuition increase, and so I was not surprised to look out my office window on 24 April 2002 to see a wave of white coats making their way from the medical school to my office. I greeted the students, saying I regretted that my office was not large enough to invite all of them in, but that if they wanted to identify representatives to join me for a conversation, I would welcome the opportunity to talk with them. They did so and I sat down with their newly identified spokespersons. I indicated that I knew they were concerned about tuition increases and I looked forward to hearing from them, but that I hoped they would answer a question for me. Informing them that the public paid about 85 per cent of the costs of their education while their individual tuition payments covered about 15 per cent, I asked them why they thought the public share should be higher than 85 per cent and their individual shares less than 15 per cent.

This visit demonstrated to me that students are not aware of the extent of the public contribution to their education. Their families and the general public cannot be expected to know more. What is most striking, though, is the absence of evidence and informed discussion at every level in which the subject of tuition is discussed, and in particular at decision-making levels within government and often universities themselves. A lack of information is not the reason; there have been several studies, commissions, and reports over the past half century.[1] But this impressive body of work has not produced considered public policy. Indeed, when it comes to the subject of tuition, we do not have policy so much as we have behaviours.

Of all the Canadian writing on the subject, none is more important than David Stager's *Focus on Fees*.[2] Though published in 1989, it remains germane today because it establishes a baseline for comparators before and after that year, and because Stager's narrative is as compelling today as it was a quarter of a century ago. Referring to the 1970s and 1980s in Ontario he wrote, "The government's position on student fees has evolved from complete university autonomy to complete government control. This occurred with no change in the universities' legal authority to determine their fees nor in the legislative framework concerning the government's budgetary powers. More importantly, the evolution of tuition fee policy was not carefully deliberated; rather it occurred in response to a variety of short-term political circumstances and pressures."[3]

This observation is not limited to Ontario and it is important for two reasons. First, the evolution from autonomy to control disregarded the authority of university boards to establish tuition rates. Considering that the government grant and tuition are the major fiscal instruments for operating a university, when governments control both, what role is there for a board to exercise authority and take responsibility for its financial affairs? Second, and related to the first, what is the incentive for people highly competent in financial matters to serve on boards of governors if their collective wisdom in financial affairs, including determining the university's revenue needs from tuition, is pre-empted by government decree? This is a serious governance matter. Boards of governors in Canada have significant numbers of insider members: university officers, faculty, students, and others who might be seen as having interests to protect or advance. If boards are to be trusted for their financial oversight, it is essential that there be able and independent people from outside the university who constitute a majority of the voting members of the board. Considering that outsiders typically serve without remuneration, theirs is public service. If their wisdom in financial matters is not recognized and accommodated, it will be more difficult to attract people of the needed calibre. In this sense, tuition controls work against good governance.

The absence of deliberation and the prominence of short-term political circumstances and pressures is also a salient point. Attention is rarely focused on whether possible or stated reasons for controlling tuition are compelling. Do controls materially advance accessibility? Have tuitions been skyrocketing? Have universities been irresponsible in relying excessively on tuition to compensate for revenue shortfalls from other sources? Does the public interest in university education so far outweigh the private interest that a new balance between public and private sources of revenue should be struck? Can we anticipate the emergence of a shift in policy emphasis in favour of advanced education such that we can anticipate that it will receive higher public investment? These are important questions, and it is in the answers to them that we should find a rationale for controls or for their absence.

Accessibility is the most prominent rationale for controls, though "accessibility is not so much a singular policy as it is a collection of socio-economic objectives"[4] that require a collection of public policies, only one of which is a policy on tuition fees. A half-century ago, accessibility in terms of the expansion of the system was emphasized to accommodate demand growth attributable to the post-war baby boom, income increases, and the association of university graduation with higher income.[5] Later in the century, accessibility in terms of equal opportunity was emphasized, particularly as it applied to minority groups, but taking into account lower-income people too. Among Stager's conclusions on the subject are these:

- Given the strong influence of the family and social influences, the elimination of tuition altogether would be unlikely to affect university enrolment very much, because tuition represents a small part of the cost (living expenses, books and supplies, transportation, and forgone income are far greater), and because of the many other factors that influence a student's decision.[6]
- "The level of parents' education is perhaps the strongest single influence on a student's decision whether to continue to post-secondary education and especially whether to take a university program."[7]
- Expansion in institutions and great expansion of student assistance programs have not appreciably increased participation rates of lower-income students in Canada or other western countries.[8]

Although these conclusions were drawn in 1989, there is no reason to believe that developments since then would yield substantial differences. What we have seen since 1989 is the evolution of provincial approaches to the tuition issue that vary in detail but feature a common bundle of tuition controls and attempts to compensate universities for those controls. In Newfoundland and Labrador, fees were rolled back between 2002 and 2005 and have been frozen since, and Memorial University has received substantial increases in provincial grants, in part in recognition of the rollback and cuts.[9] In the Maritime provinces there has been a combination of freezes, caps on increases, and grants intended to compensate universities for these measures. Quebec has a long history of freezing tuition that has seen fees frozen for Quebec students in thirty-four of the past forty-four years. In Ontario, fees were frozen from 2004 to 2006, again with some compensatory funding and new investments targeted at creating places for sixty thousand additional college and university students by 2015. In Manitoba, freezes for the first decade of this century have been followed by increases held to the rate of inflation. Saskatchewan has seen announced freezes and caps but with understandings reached in advance about levels of compensatory grants.[10] After setting and resetting tuitions in 2005–7, Alberta now limits increases to increases in the Alberta Consumer Price Index. British Columbia experienced freezes from 1992 to 1994 and again from 1996 to 2002, with caps since 2005 linked to the British Columbia Consumer Price Index.

In the midst of these developments, Bob Rae was appointed advisor to the Ontario premier and the minister of training, colleges, and universities. His broad mandate included a request for his advice on an appropriate sharing of the costs of post-secondary education among government, students, and the private sector. He wrote, "The notion that higher education is some kind of nationalized industry, where the price of everything is set by central planners in an office at Queen's Park, is out of place in the modern world. We shall not achieve greater autonomy, flexibility and competition within the system – all desirable goals – so long as all tuition decisions are made centrally."[11]

Rae was clear that both government and universities have a role in tuition: "The government should not set tuition levels but should establish the regulatory framework that ensures predictability, transparency and affordability for students. The institutions must clearly retain ultimate responsibility for tuition levels of individual programs. In doing so, the regulatory framework should require that – in the context of multi-year plans – the institutions publicly commit to and be held to account for both the tangible quality improvements that students will see for increases in tuition, and adequate financial support for students in need."[12]

Rae was clearly of the view that tuition controls do not advance accessibility and that students should pay part of the costs. "Otherwise we would be asking taxpayers who don't go [to university] to subsidize those who do."[13] He devoted much of his report to financial assistance for students, a subject to which we shall turn shortly.

Six years after the Rae Report, the Higher Education Quality Council of Ontario released its issue paper "Tuition Fee Policy Options for Ontario."[14] To the question on the impact of tuition fees on accessibility and persistence, "the answer ... is clear: Canadian research finds no consistent relationship between tuition fees and PSE [post-secondary education] participation and persistence rates."[15] Ontario had the highest average undergraduate tuition fee in Canada; it also had the highest university participation rate.[16] The evidence was also clear on the private benefits of post-secondary education: "Education provides graduates with higher average annual earnings and lower unemployment rates, and this relationship varies consistently with levels of education. High school graduates earn more on average than those without a high school diploma; college diploma holders earn more on average than high school graduates; those with a Bachelor's degree earn more on average than college diploma holders; and those with professional and postgraduate degrees have the highest average earnings."[17]

And, the paper continues, the differences are significant,[18] even more so when we take into account the fact that actual tuition costs are less than fees reported by Statistics Canada. The cost is less than the sticker price because of tax and other offsetting credits and programs. In Ontario, "nominal tuition fee increases since 2000 have been almost completely offset by the combined effects of inflation and other tax credits."[19] Nationally the picture is similar. In *Beyond the Sticker Shock: A Closer Look at Canadian Tuition Fees*,[20] Usher and Duncan reported in 2008 that the real cost of post-secondary education was effectively the same as in 2000, with tuition increases effectively offset by tax rebates and other credits. Some provinces had experienced a net real cost decline.[21]

Notwithstanding the evidence running against the argument that low tuition increases accessibility, a higher public investment in post-secondary education could alter the public good / private good balance in favour of the former. It is unlikely that such an investment will take place. Apart from current restraint and the unpredictability of the economic cycle generally, public health care has been winning the priorities contest against all provincial public spending competitors, including post-secondary education. And its demands for public dollars are insatiable.

The main fiscal problem with health care is that its costs are rising faster than the revenue of any government in Canada. Consider Ontario: between 1997–98 and 2002–03, government spending on health-care increased by

42 percent while government revenue only went up by 31 percent. Because health spending is growing at a faster rate than government revenue, it is consuming a larger and larger share of the public spending pie. Prior to 1994–1995 the Ontario Government spent about 32 percent of its budget on health care. By 2003–2004 it accounted for 39 percent of the budget. Currently, 46% of Ontario's budget is spent on health care and without major changes, it is estimated that by 2030 it will consume a whopping 80% of the budget.[22]

Simply, public health care "is squeezing out funding for other important programs,"[23] a fiscal environment that is unlikely to see a reordering of priorities in the foreseeable future in favour of post-secondary education, or anything else, for that matter.

Of course additional funding could come from Ottawa. The Rae Report opined that "the federal government has been avoiding its responsibilities towards higher education"[24] and called for a dedicated federal transfer to the provinces for higher education.[25] This change is unlikely for some of the same reasons that apply to the provinces, including continuing and growing federal expenditures on health care.[26] In addition, the federal government is unlikely to reverse changes in policy since 1995 that were seen to be necessary to improve Canada's competitiveness and innovation.

Yet the impulse to freeze or control tuition persists. In Saskatchewan, a 2007 report authored by a New Democratic Party MLA[27] recommended not only that tuition be frozen but that it be reduced, and his report was the inspiration for his party's promises in provincial elections in 2007 and 2011 to freeze tuition. But it was in Quebec that the issue was most prominent, and on this occasion, the whole country was paying attention.

In 2011, in a province in which tuition freezes were the norm, the Government of Quebec proposed tuition increases over five years of $325 a year. By 2016 tuition in the province would continue to be the lowest or second-lowest in Canada[28] and, according to premier Jean Charest, would see Quebec students paying about 17 per cent of the cost of their education.[29] On 10 November 2011 the premier's proposal was greeted initially by a demonstration of twenty thousand students at his Montreal office, and the protest escalated from there. By early 2012, classes were boycotted and students were in the streets, some engaging in episodic violence resulting in injuries and arrests. The number of protesters increased, initially to the tens of thousands and, at times, to well over a hundred thousand. Some demonstrators or bystanders were injured. Bridges were blocked and other public and business facilities were damaged or disrupted. The protests spread from Montreal to other parts of the province.

The demonstrations attracted sympathizers, including major Quebec labour unions, who pinned the movement's symbolic red felt square to their lapels. They did not capture public opinion in Quebec or in the rest of Canada, though there was a high level of awareness of the protests across the country.[30]

In early May, government and student leaders reached an agreement to end the boycott of classes, which included a government commitment to spread the tuition increase over seven years, not five, and a further commitment to strike a committee with student input to look for savings in university budgets. But the agreement was flawed because the student leaders would not recommend it to their followers and it was not ratified. Days later, Minister of Education Line Beauchamp resigned from her post and left politics, and the government introduced emergency legislation to end the crisis.[31] The legislation passed in the National Assembly but it did not end the protests, and on 23 May more than five hundred protesters were arrested in Montreal, a single night record since the protests began.

With classes over and the school year suspended, the protests receded as summer began, and by the time it ended, Quebec had a new Parti Québécois government, which acted on day one of its mandate to cancel the proposed tuition increases, as well as the emergency legislation that had both broadened and strengthened the protest.

The immediate consequence was that Quebec universities had to absorb the burden of the cancelled increases. McGill principal Heather Munroe-Blum described the impact: "What this does is deepen dramatically what was already a very substantial hole in the funding of Quebec's universities ... We've just taken a giant step towards increasing the deficits of Quebec's universities, over and above what is close to a $700-million annual gap in funding."[32]

Beyond aggravating immediate university budget pressures, the outcome of the Quebec tuition protest will be felt for years. After forcing the Charest government to make major concessions as it reeled from the impact of the demonstrations, the Marois government gave the protesters a complete victory and encouraged them to think about next steps, including the abolition of tuition. The episode was also an affirmation of interventionist government, as one administration legislated tuition increases and another cancelled them. It is unlikely that any Quebec government, in the foreseeable future, will accord more deference in tuition matters to the province's universities. It is also unlikely that government will itself raise tuition significantly, thereby courting a repetition of the protests of 2011 and 2012.

The successful protest was not the "triumph of justice and equity" celebrated by student leader Martine Desjardins.[33] On the contrary, writes Pierre Fortin of the University of Quebec at Montreal, free tuition, and by extension excessive control of tuition, would create an injustice.[34] Making taxpayers pay for tuition control and containment at universities may be a popular appeal, but the result would be large increases in tax rates. The problem with this, according to Fortin, is not only the magnitude of the tax increases needed, but neglect of the principle of horizontal equity by treating non-graduates and graduates identically, when it is the latter who are the beneficiaries. Moreover, Fortin argues, it ignores Quebec's fiscal reality, including the need not to be too far out of step in its tax rates with its North American neighbours.

University tuition in Quebec is now effectively frozen, perhaps more frozen than ever, thus setting the stage for the next round of protests. As Fortin argues,[35] the real costs of university education continue to increase, which means that the students' relative contribution to those costs continues to go down. Eventually there must be a correction to address the under-financing of universities, and the freeze – if it continues – would make the correction difficult and more likely to produce a repetition of the social upheaval we witnessed in 2011 and 2012.

It is important that tuition behaviours be replaced by tuition policy. Given the political differences among the provinces and the variation in their fiscal capacities, coast-to-coast policy agreement is unlikely. But that should not preclude the effort. No provincial jurisdiction can claim disinterest in what the others are doing. Young Canadians should be encouraged to view their university options broadly. We should prompt them to consider their university years as an opportunity to see more of Canada. Reasonable compatibility among the provinces in tuition and student aid policies would make this easier.

At the core of the tuition issue are two challenges. The first is to identify a compelling approach to the respective public and private gains and benefits that flow from university education. The second is to identify the kind of financial support policies that would ensure that accessibility would not suffer and instead would be improved.

Some of the public and private gains can be quantified, but not all of them. The issue is part economics and part philosophy. What do we want to assert as a common and credible value of university education that takes account of public and private, quantifiable and unquantifiable benefits? One possibility is that the individual and the public benefit in roughly equal measure: the individual benefits as much as society, and vice versa, and we should set the public/private gains at 50:50.[36]

All universities would have to be able to identify the per student costs of offering each of its programs. Eight provinces have two or more universities, and the costs of common programs would be averaged. Each provincial government would commit to providing each university in the province with 50 per cent of its average costs by program. In provinces with only one university, 50 per cent of actual costs would be available, and the remaining 50 per cent would presumptively be charged as tuition.

For the sake of argument, let's develop the idea further. In meeting the needs of universities to secure 100 per cent of their costs, governments should not be prescriptive about tuitions they must charge. Universities should decide for themselves where they wish to be with respect to average program costs; they should not be drawn inevitably to them and therefore to a common "average" program. A particular university may decide it wishes to commit to a particular program – or to all its programs, for that matter – more than its presumptive 50 per cent share of average program costs. Its program in history, say, may be the best or one of the best available, and the university may wish to commit resources necessary to keep it at that level or to aspire even higher, and to assume responsibility for the higher than average costs required to support it. The converse should also be possible. A university may find that its costs are less than the average for one or more of its programs. Perhaps it has efficiencies in program delivery that are not shared by other institutions; perhaps the program is not among its priorities and therefore commands fewer resources. These differences must be left to the universities to determine and to set tuition accordingly. They will be subject to the discipline of the market in doing so, and students will have a choice about the kind of program they wish to attend, its profile, reputation, and aspirations.

For such an approach to work, there are prerequisites. First, universities must be committed to identify all program costs, including an appropriate measure to ensure maintenance and renewal of facilities. Second, they must be open to periodic assessments of their programs and to making university plans and priorities, together with program quality assessments, public and available to all applicants. Third, universities (along with governments) must reimagine their financial assistance policies as an essential foundation of tuition policy.

Governments must recognize that all costs must be included, including a measure for deferred maintenance, a growing problem at Canadian universities and one that thus far has been avoided more than it has been addressed. They must also work with universities – it is a joint responsibility – to ensure that a framework for financial assistance is in place so that that no qualified student is precluded from attending university for financial reasons. And they must commit to leaving it to the universities to establish tuitions for the programs they offer.

Let us turn, now, to the matter of financial assistance for students. As important as the subject is, we should acknowledge what the evidence has borne out for years: that neither tuition levels nor financial assistance programs are the most important determinants of decisions to continue education to post-secondary levels. The absence of parental participation in post-secondary education, and the influence of parents and others close to those facing the decision, are more important. We should reflect on the growing significance of this fact in an age when employment prospects for those without post-secondary education are poor and diminishing. The growing value of a degree for career prospects has been evident in labour market signals for many years. A young person's decision to forgo post-secondary education of some kind is in nearly all cases a bad decision, both for that person and for the rest of society who are deprived of the benefits of a decision to the contrary, and who may have to shoulder its social costs later on.

Our society has to do better in educating its members about the critical importance of education, and the disadvantage incurred by those who eschew its benefits. All of the good work done by guidance counsellors, and by primary and high school teachers and administrators, to advise and encourage their students to continue their studies is insufficient when their influence is attenuated by ignorance about just how important the decision is. We need to broaden the discussion of accessibility beyond tuition and financial assistance, beyond capacity and quality, to include the social influences of parents and others in the decisions that young people make about their futures. We need to educate larger numbers of our fellow citizens about the importance of education.

In turning our attention to financial assistance we are focusing on those predisposed to continue their studies but who feel unable to do so for financial reasons. Our goal should be to ensure that no one falls into this category, that all who would continue on to post-secondary studies and who are qualified to do so have that opportunity. Given the discussion of tuition above, what are the implications of this goal for individuals, for universities, and for their public sponsors, particularly governments?

We should begin by asking what principles should guide financial assistance for university students. I believe there are three: transparency, full cost inclusion, and income-contingent repayment conditions. Transparency in this context means that programs should be widely publicized, readily understood, and unburdened by numerous or complex regulations. For example, the time and effort spent on determining loan eligibility through family income thresholds is not productive. Family income is not always easily determined, and income may not account for all resources available to a family. In addition, regardless of income, a family may not be committed to the post-secondary education of one of its members. Further, the composition and durability of families is less predictable than it once was and should not be counted upon in making judgments of this kind.

The second principle – inclusion of full and reasonable costs in determining resource needs – recognizes that in Canada living costs typically exceed tuition and related charges and often are more of a barrier to accessibility than instructional costs. Large numbers of students must leave home to attend university, and it should not be assumed that those who attend university in their home towns will be living at home at little or no cost to themselves.

The third principle is repayment of most needs-based financial assistance, but on an income-contingent basis. On the present argument the public is prepared to fund 50 per cent of the costs to universities of mounting their programs. The even share of costs reflects the public benefit anticipated from an individual's decision to attend university and would not be repayable, but an income-contingent loan to cover some or all of the remaining costs should be repaid when permitted by employment income. In effect the public has made an investment that, if it turns out to be a good one, should be repaid.

There is support in the literature and in policy for financial assistance repayable on an income-contingent basis. The Rae Report considered issues and improvements in the current mixture of loans and grants, but Rae was intrigued by the idea of a public investment in upfront costs of students in need, with repayment later by what he called a "graduate benefit."[37] He found arguments against income-sensitive repayment "unpersuasive"[38] and urged the development of a new framework for financial assistance for post-secondary students.[39] The Higher Education Quality Council of Ontario considered income contingent loans to be an alternative to current practices: "There are many variations of such schemes but a common feature is that debt repayment obligations are tied to income after graduation as reported to tax authorities. There is usually a minimum income level below which there are no repayment obligations. Above this minimum level, repayments increase as income increases, in absolute amounts but also frequently as a percentage of family income. There is usually a maximum income figure beyond which full debt plus carrying charges must be repaid."[40] The council noted that loan repayment options of this kind are found in Australia and the United Kingdom.

Assuming the principles to be sound, we should consider their implications. With respect to transparency, we must recognize that the principle works two ways. The basis on which financial assistance is available should be well known and understood. So too should be an understanding that deferral means precisely that: deferral and not exemption. If students understand that, in return for present access to university education, they will be obliged in due course to repay its cost, they will be more likely to do all they can to contain present cost in the interest of manageable repayment later on.

Cumulatively the tuition proposal and principles-based financial assistance invite a reimagining of the complex web of government and university programs now in place. The changes would free universities to rethink the focus, goals, and mechanisms of policies developed so far. Canadian universities commit $3 billion per year to student financial assistance. A change on the scale proposed here could lead universities to reconsider their scholarship programs and needs-based grants and loans. It is possible that it could lead some universities to redeploy resources now directed to student aid to other programs designed to enhance the student experience, including study abroad or in a different region of Canada, to bring more of the best international students to Canada, and to provide opportunities for undergraduates to participate in research and in service learning.

The existence of a principles-based approach to tuition and financial assistance should lead universities to ensure that those principles are respected in their internal policies. If the relative public and private benefit is appropriately reflected in equal public and private contributions to university costs, the institutions should not feel pressure to provide ever-growing monies to assist students with tuition and living costs; they would now have loans repayable on an income-contingent basis to supplement their own resources for this purpose. Universities might deploy their monies more creatively in ways that assist in achieving other goals such as those mentioned above: study abroad or in a different region of Canada; bringing international students to Canada; and opportunities for undergraduates to participate in research and in service learning.

The cost of this approach must also be considered, and here we must concede that the information is incomplete. Three factors are important, though. First, the approach is best conceived as an investment, as distinct from an expenditure. Second, comparable programs in other countries have not been deterred by the anticipation of costs that are prohibitive. Third, and most important, factoring in the cost of current programs – credits, loans, grants, and bursaries – that would be redundant if the approach described here were adopted, would make it more affordable.

For example, tax credits and grants that reduce the sticker price of instructional costs could be eliminated, freeing resources now committed to them to be available in accordance with the principles described here.

Finally, it is apparent that implementation of this approach would require federal-provincial collaboration in rethinking current policies, abandoning some, and substituting for them a principle-based program for paying the upfront reasonable costs for qualified students seeking to access university education, who assume an income-contingent repayment obligation.

A collaborative effort that is broadly inclusive of all or most provinces as well as the federal government may not be likely, but it should be possible. Surely there are few voices that would claim satisfaction with current approaches to tuition, financial assistance for students, and the broader accessibility issues in Canadian post-secondary education. If there is common agreement that we need to do better, identification of the ways in which we can do better should not be far behind. This chapter outlines one possible approach, beginning with a principle-based apportionment of public/private benefits and outlining its implications for funding universities and financial assistance for students. Whether the approach is compelling in comparison with current practice or other possible approaches should be tested by discussion and debate among governments and institutions.

Canadians know of the attention devoted to their health care. Less attention is devoted to post-secondary education, even though it has long been accepted that good education supports healthy lives and thereby the containment of health-care costs. More and better public policy attention to post-secondary education should be seen as supporting other policy goals rather than as competing with them. In the post-industrial world, knowledge and understanding are the keys to successful lives and successful countries. Universities are in the knowledge and understanding business, and access to them is more important than ever. In the interest of their individual and collective futures, Canadians need to do a better job of understanding, debating, and resolving access issues.

Chapter Four

Yes Minister: On Government Engagement, Academic Freedom, and Collective Advocacy

Shortly before the end of my first year in office I travelled to Regina to meet with the minister whose Cabinet portfolio included universities. He scolded me because an opposition member of the legislative assembly had been seated in the front row of the platform party at a recent convocation ceremony, and accused me of "working with the opposition" because I briefed opposition legislators as well as government members on the issues faced by the university. Later the same minister informed me that he would be attending a meeting of our board of governors. Upon his arrival at this meeting he took a seat between me and other board members, with his back to me. His speech emphasized his responsibility for universities, and he announced that henceforth he intended to have a direct relationship with the board of governors. It was clear that he did not intend that I would have a leadership role in that relationship.

Occasionally a board must act as a buffer between its president and a minister, and on this occasion it did so by inviting the minister to direct his remarks to me. It was not prepared to entertain his attempt to establish a relationship, bypassing me, with the board, and to assert that he had executive authority for the university: presidents do not report to ministers.

But – and it is a large but – they do have obligations to them, which make the relationship as nuanced as it is important. The minister is responsible to her government to ensure that its policies that relate to universities are properly executed. And she is well placed to influence those policies: she can be an advocate in support of university plans or a voice that diminishes them. She can be influential in a decision to squeeze budgets or to augment them. She is appropriately thanked and accorded deference, or greeted with rebuttal, as the occasion demands. And there are many different occasions. Ministers and their governments may be publicly lauded one week for facilitating a major initiative, and criticized the next for inadequate operating budget support. The dynamic between presidents and ministers requires understandings on the part of both of their different offices and responsibilities; it also requires empathy by each for the constraints and demands on the other.

These understandings begin with recognition that the agendas of universities and governments overlap but do not match. One illustration in my meeting with the minister was his concern that I was briefing members of the opposition on issues facing the university. His reservation, I believe, was that I was doing so in order to provide grist for question period that might put him on the defensive in the legislature. My purpose, as I explained to him, was to educate all public officials, government or opposition, federal, provincial, and municipal, on what was at stake on the University of Saskatchewan campus, and why it was important to all of them. But our differences only began there.

In general, provincial ministers want universities to educate their constituents at a price they can influence, if not control. They are not particularly interested in faculty, except those that provide essential clinical services. They have little interest in research, and none in deferred maintenance, the removal of asbestos, or the replacement of a boiler that has just failed. Nor is a future vision likely to intrigue let alone excite them. And they don't want protests, demonstrations, or incidents that result in a call to action on their part. Presidents, if they are doing their jobs, have to pay attention to students, faculty, staff, the present and future of the university and its infrastructure, and the external constituencies on which the future well-being of the university depends. Despite their differences, ministers and presidents must listen to one another. Neither is in a position to dictate to the other.

A university can cope with an inauspicious or even negative relationship between its president and a minister, though not easily. A constructive ongoing conversation is important to ensure that governments and universities have the requisite understanding of one another and of current issues and concerns. Rapid turnover of ministers can diminish the conversation (ministerial changes averaged nearly one a year in my first eight years as president). So can a lack of understanding of respective roles or indiscretion with the media and public. A president and the responsible provincial Cabinet minister should have trust in

one another and must communicate with one another if the relationship between university and government is to be a mature one. Mutual
expectations must be respected and met if the relationship is to be an
excellent one.

What are these mutual expectations? What should universities
expect of governments and vice versa? Consider, first, provincial governments, which have constitutional responsibility for education. They
should provide resources commensurate with university contributions
to the public good, be clear about government priorities and limitations, and respect the universities' governance and autonomy. The discussion in chapter 3 recognizes that there is both a public and private
interest in an individual's decision to complete a university education,
and that in general these interests are appropriately expressed by equal
contributions to the costs incurred by the universities in providing that
education. The remainder should be provided by tuition, provided
that loans repayable on an income-contingent basis are available. Government support consistent with this approach to public and private
good is essential if our universities are to remain substantially public
institutions.

The trajectory over recent decades is a decline in the per student
public support for the operating costs of universities.[1] Sometimes the
trajectory straightens out, and it may even turn up for a time. But the
long-term direction down is clear.[2] If this continues for an extended
period of time, it is not hyperbole to speak of the privatization of university education. If it is fair that the public interest in an individual's
decision to complete a degree or certificate be recognized equally with
the private interest, provincial government contributions falling below
that share constitute a shirking of provincial government responsibility.
If this happens, and it should be recognized as a public policy choice
to let it happen, government must accept the consequences. The most
immediate one is an increase in the private share of the costs.

University contributions to the public good include research as well
as teaching. Here the funding arrangements vary but, whatever they
may be, universities must recover their full direct and indirect costs,
which should not include a contribution from tuition. Students do not
attend university in order to subsidize research, though they have been
doing so, because institutions have been unable to recover their full
costs from research agencies and sponsors. When the sponsors are provincial governments, they must be prepared to pay full costs, though
their engagement in university research is not limited to exclusive

sponsorship. Research partnerships may include federal and provincial governments, industry, and other collaborators. It is important that provinces remain open to participating in these partnerships, with financial contributions commensurate with their engagement.

An understanding of government priorities and limitations is also important to universities, and they should expect clarity on them. Governments are large and complex organizations, but so are universities, and they need to be able to anticipate and plan on more than a reactive basis. University leaders know that meeting the always increasing costs of health care is the top priority of provincial governments, and that education will yield before this and sometimes other social and political budget imperatives. This too is a public policy choice. But if universities are treated like annual supplicants, waiting uncertainly in line behind health care and other more immediate priorities for government decisions that they cannot anticipate, they cannot plan effectively. For this reason, too, relationships and communication are important, because they can foster the informal messages that can lead to more informed and timely decisions.

The third expectation that universities can reasonably have of governments is that they will respect autonomy and governance. Of course, for them to be respected, they must be understood. Autonomy does not mean – as some in the university would like it to mean – that government writes cheques, then stands back and watches. Governments can be too deferential as well as too interfering, and the challenge is to find the right level of engagement. Doing so requires them to recognize that trusteeship, oversight, and administration of a university's plans and day-to-day activities have been entrusted to its governing bodies and senior administration. The president is responsible to the board of governors or its equivalent, not to the minister. The board is also responsible for appointing a president and for oversight of the institution's finances, property, and business affairs. Its academic affairs are in the hands of a senate or similar body by whatever name. Its faculty have academic freedom in their teaching and scholarship.

Expectations are reciprocal, and governments have some of their own. Universities expect to be understood by governments, and it would help if more university people understood the burdens of governing. "Government is a very tough world, full of pressures, tensions and contradictions. A new government begins with strong policy commitments, but the pressures of political influence and events are highly distracting. The work is complex and unrelenting, while expectations

are so high they can rarely be met and scrutiny is extensive and unfor-
giving. In some ways it is an impossible task."[3]

The variety of talents and personalities in politics presents further
challenges. "The term politician seems to suggest a class of people who
have something in common. However, about the only thing that all politicians have in common is that they are actively engaged, at a particular
moment, in electoral politics. Otherwise, they are a highly varied lot. It
is doubtful that the people in any other occupational group – doctors,
teachers, electricians, insurance agents – are more diverse than are the
people in politics."[4]

For former Saskatchewan premier Allan Blakeney, the task of governing brought to mind the mythical Sisyphus, though instead of his inter-
minable task of rolling a stone up a mountain only to have it roll down
again for the manoeuvre to be repeated, governments have stones regularly deposited in their backpacks until eventually they collapse under
their weight.[5]

Among those depositing stones in the backpacks is the official opposition. University presidents do not have an official opposition – just
unofficial ones – but they need to understand what it means to have
a political adversary with the constitutional responsibility to oppose
what government does. Mistakes, controversies, or indiscretions – real,
perceived, or imagined – are cannon fodder for daily question period
or denunciation in the media. And the government-in-waiting is aided
by a media "whose coverage tends to focus simplistically on heroes
and villains, or winners and losers … The media distrust government
and tend to look for problems and negatives."[6] The result is a "gotcha"
style of public life and discourse in which the focus is on avoiding
mistakes more than it is on policy development and maturation. This
means that immediate concerns attract more attention than do longer-
term ones, and of course the culture clash is unavoidable: universities
must plan for their futures, and governments must address the immediate concerns that may put them in jeopardy. Navigating these differences requires that they be understood.

The pressures that bear upon politicians make it all the more important to be familiar with the public service. These are the people who
develop policy options and advise politicians, and some of them are
more influential than the politicians they serve. They are privy to the
government's views on issues and people, and they are knowledgeable
about areas in which they have responsibility. The best of them are good
advisors, not only of government but of those who seek its engagement

and support. University leaders need to know and have access to these people and to earn their confidence.

Universities sometimes complain that governments prioritize schools and colleges over them. Certainly they may devote more attention to them, and for a number of reasons. They have more authority over schools and colleges than they do over universities, and in the case of colleges, missions are seen to be more compatible with the shorter time horizons of governments. "The oft-held view is that investing in shorter-term training in technology produces better economic payoffs than does a general higher education such as a Bachelor of Arts ... The best available evidence does not, in fact, support the superiority of shorter term technical training ... but here, as in so many places, the facts are less significant than are public beliefs."[7]

In addition there is the "love–hate relationship that governments have with universities."[8] Levin refers to a 1991 study in which Stuart Smith reported strong and widely held views of Ontario politicians and public servants that universities were "elitist, smug, unwilling to change, unproductive and expensive."[9] But governments also need universities to educate students, maintain high skill levels, support the learned professions, and produce useful ideas and potential products.[10] So the love–hate relationship – if that is what it is – will endure, and perhaps improve with greater mutual understanding. Perhaps it already has done so.

Understanding the burdens and attitudes of politicians and public servants is vital to successful university-government relations. So too is responsiveness to reasonable expectations of government on mission, quality, and accountability. Identifying the range and scope of its activities is not solely a university's business. Because it has implications for public finances, government must be involved in and ultimately approve the programs a university offers. Of course mandate is partly historical and in established universities has developed over a long time with either government support or acquiescence. It is not changeable quickly or on a whim, and it should not be. And governments must leave to the universities the question of how their mandates are met. But ultimately in a public system mandates are changeable, and in the case of new institutions may be prescribed.

Clark et al.[11] describe the post-secondary education design choices faced by all jurisdictions: the nature and extent of institutional differentiation; the academic credentials to be awarded by each institution; differences in emphases on teaching and research; the relationships among institutions, particularly with respect to student mobility; how to group institutions for the purposes of administration and funding allocation decisions; whether to centralize authority or devolve it to individual campuses; and whether to allow for private institutions.[12] The choices are more complicated in a federal state such as Canada, where both provinces and Ottawa have interests in post-secondary education, albeit different interests or emphases. "A striking feature of the Ontario university system in comparison with other public systems of comparable size has been the lack of mandated institutional differentiation by mission, function, areas of study, educational philosophy, or approach to program delivery."[13]

There are differences in numbers of graduate programs and in program mix. And there are differences "in character, traditions and institutional culture,"[14] but there are not "differences in mission and role that are the result of deliberate public policy decisions." Their absence inspired the observation that Ontario "does not have a provincial strategy for post-secondary education."[15]

Such a strategy could be developed by a provincial agency responsible for oversight of system development, but neither in Ontario nor in much of the rest of Canada have these agencies existed over time or had the authority the task would require. Government could do the task itself, or rely on the institutions themselves or through an organization such as the Council of Ontario Universities, or rely on competitive market forces, to differentiate and locate themselves in relation to other institutions in the province.[16] For a variety of reasons these approaches have not worked. In particular, reliance on market forces requires that the system be "relatively free of constraints on the ability of institutions to respond to new opportunities and pressures,"[17] which Ontario is not, because of the regulation of price through tuition and approval requirements for new programs.

The picture across the country varies. In Alberta, in 2007 the responsible ministry developed six categories of institutional designation: comprehensive academic and research, baccalaureate and applied studies, polytechnics, comprehensive community (such as community colleges), independent (private) academic institutions, and specialized arts and culture institutions. For the past half-century, governments in Alberta and British Columbia have been "modifying and reshaping the design of their post-secondary systems in relation to changes in provincial needs and circumstances."[18]

Since the Quiet Revolution of the 1960s in Quebec, governments have been involved in developing post-secondary structure and oversight.

The CEGEPS[19] and the University of Quebec system are its principal manifestations, and in general government has been more activist in post-secondary education than in Ontario, no doubt in part because of the rapid and state-inspired development of the sector in Quebec, as compared to its more evolutionary development in Ontario.

In 1997 Manitoba created a Council on Post-Secondary Education with a coordination and oversight mandate, though it has not been active in either. Saskatchewan had one in the decade following the creation of the University of Regina, but it was discontinued and not replaced. There are no comparable bodies in New Brunswick and Nova Scotia, though in the former a new Research and Innovation Council is charged with increasing collaboration among universities, industry, and government.[20] A recent report in Nova Scotia acknowledged that a redesign of the province's post-secondary sector would result in a reduction in the high number of institutions relative to the size of the province but ruled out system overhaul in favour of modest restructuring. The issues do not arise in Newfoundland and Labrador, and in Prince Edward Island, each of which has one university only.

In summary, Ontario is closer to what Clark et al. describe as a homogeneity model of institutional differentiation, with other provinces at varying distances from it but still a long way from a heterogeneity model.[21] Their proposal for Ontario is to create new institutions focused on undergraduate education, taking measures necessary to ensure that this specialization "is not regarded as a temporary stage on the road to eventually becoming comprehensive institutions like the others."[22] Clark et al. envisage that the number and locations of these new institutions would be responsive to student demand and that anticipated growth in Toronto would make it home to at least two of them. They further propose "that all new publicly assisted degree-granting institutions in the province would be of this type for the foreseeable future."[23]

Clark et al. may have the diagnosis right but the remedy wrong. Primarily undergraduate universities will have research missions too, and important initiatives to improve undergraduate education have emanated from medical-doctoral universities. George Fallis agrees that undergraduate studies require greater attention, but his views on remedy are in contrast to those of Clark et al.[24] He makes a compelling case for a renewal of the social contract between society and its multiversities and, by extension, its research universities generally. His agenda[25] for this renewal includes two priorities: the recognition of the multiversity as an institution of democracy, and increased attention to undergraduate education. With respect to the latter, Fallis is not among the most severe critics of the track record; he observes that "the multiversity has proven to be a relatively hospitable home for undergraduate education."[26] But, he says, "it must be candidly admitted that the research mission of the multiversity is potentially the greatest disadvantage to undergraduate education."[27] Meeting this potential through greater attention to undergraduate studies is an idea that "has been honoured more in word than in deed."[28] His call to action is an appeal to make this a priority among the multiversities' broad responsibilities, rather than to diminish that commitment through the creation of new, specialized undergraduate institutions.

Responsiveness to government and public expectations on quality will be more important in the future than in the past when judgments about quality – if made at all – were more discrete and impressionistic than they now are. "Our age has many forces that are creating a competitive hierarchy among multiversities, both within countries and across countries."[29] The competition is explicit, measurable, and public, and the task of locating Canadian universities within the hierarchy is one that must draw on national and local expectations of governments and communities of all kinds, as well as institutional capacities and ambitions. The question of what we expect of ourselves is an important public policy question, and it should be debated and addressed as one.

It is not an easy debate. There are no ground rules, and there are many participants whose motivations vary and whose candour cannot be assumed. But it should be a welcome debate, one that brings clarity to the issue of differentiation and to the expectations that universities and governments have of themselves and one another. In our federal state, it is a debate that must take place locally, although, as we have seen, it is influenced by evolving national policies, particularly in research.

University presidents have a unique role in leading this debate. It is a condition necessary for success in their offices that they offer a compelling vision of their institutions for ten and twenty years into the future. That vision has to be tested within the academy and against the expectations of governments, communities, partners, and supporters of all kinds. And it must be tested against a backdrop of path dependency, which accounts for where their institutions find themselves today, and the odds for and against altering their paths to meet new expectations.

The advantage of this debate is that it compels participants to declare themselves and to be complicit in change or defenders of a status quo. It should lead to a consensus on expectations within universities and the external communities on which they depend. Canada has many good universities and some excellent ones. Do we as Canadians expect our multiversities to be among the best in the world? Are they now? How do we ensure that our best universities sustain and improve quality, while others are brought to a higher standard? What are the responsibilities of the universities themselves, and of their supporting communities, in meeting expectations? These are the public policy questions that are at stake and, for the first time in our history, they are explicit and prominent. And they require answers.

My answers to the above questions are these: Canadians should expect their multiversities to be among the best in the world and should hold them to account for demonstrating that they are in this exclusive company, or making progress to that end. Progress here will require our multiversities, indeed our universities generally, to improve their standing, as determined both by external rankings and validated internal measures and surveys. They should ask and be asked – publicly – what the impediments and barriers are to improvement, and how they can be removed. Progress will also require governments and supportive communities to be better educated about the policies and supports that are the necessary conditions for improvement, and their roles in implementing them.

Answering these questions will lead to a greater and more explicit differentiation among our universities, and this should be welcomed. It will help students and their families in the comparisons necessary to making the best choices for them. It will help governments and others to identify policies that integrate these differences in decision-making, and it will help the universities themselves to understand what is required of them in a differentiated system, and to meet those requirements.

It is a truism to assert that governments expect universities to be accountable, and that universities expect accountability of themselves. The elements of accountability common to public institutions of all kinds are present here: financial, legal, and more broadly, political accountability for institutional standing, direction, and relationships. Topics peculiar to universities that sometimes raise questions of accountability in government and elsewhere are autonomy and academic freedom. The former has to do with the integrity of university governance and is a topic we encounter in many settings throughout this book. The latter is a fundamental value of uncertain and sometimes disputed scope that requires clarification in the interest of accountability within universities, and beyond them to governments and the general public.

My definition[30] of academic freedom is this: the freedom to teach and conduct research constrained only by (1) the professional standards of the relevant discipline, and (2) legitimate and non-discriminatory institutional requirements for organizing the academic mission. With one there is an implicit distinction between academic freedom and freedom of speech, and academic freedom is a narrower concept. Easy examples will illustrate: exponents of Holocaust denial and members of the Flat Earth Society are free to speak their minds on these subjects on the street – they have freedom of speech – but they are not entitled to claim academic freedom in defence of doing so in their classrooms and publications. The reason is that the claims fall below the professional standards of history and astronomy.

I must acknowledge rebuttal on two fronts to a constraint on academic freedom that is based on a distinction between it and freedom of speech. Critics might argue that today's heresy may be tomorrow's truth, and it might be suppressed by insisting that it may not enjoy the protection of academic freedom. Critics might also argue that all ideas are open to question, including the shape of the earth and the historical records of the Holocaust.

My response is that I agree but that neither criticism undermines the argument. An insistence on professional standards speaks to the rigour of the enquiry and not to its outcome. And while it is true that all ideas are open to question in a university, they must be questioned systematically and on the evidence, and answers must be defensible in reason. The claim that "I'm entitled to my opinion" has limited currency in an environment whose raison d'être is evidence, reason, and argument. You may indeed be entitled to your opinion, but your opinion is of no interest and garners no credit if it cannot withstand scrutiny based on reason and relevant professional standards of investigation.

The second constraint on academic freedom – legitimate and non-discriminatory institutional requirements – recognizes simply that the academic mission, like any other work, has to be organized, and it does not violate academic freedom to insist upon reasonable compliance with organizational needs like teaching according to a schedule, and adhering to collegial and administrative expectations for getting work done.

My definition is contested on broader terms, namely its grounding of academic freedom in teaching and research, thereby precluding its extension to activities and speech that are not related to these duties.[31] It is commonly argued that a faculty member is protected by academic freedom in interactions with colleagues, students, and the administration in expressing criticism of the university or any of its policies, or in offering opinions on any subject and in any setting. Moderation, civility, or professionalism are not among the requirements for the protection of academic freedom under the broad ambit claimed for it here. My response is that academic freedom exists to protect scholarly enquiry and that interactions with others, criticisms of the university or ex cathedra pronouncements may be part of or related to that mission, in which case they are protected by academic freedom. Or they may not, in which case unprofessional conduct or violations of university rules and policies can attract sanctions, as they would in any employment setting.

Accountability issues with academic freedom arise in two ways. With the first, critics are perplexed by the freedom of academics to determine so many of their professional activities, including their research programs. This criticism is not common and is easily answered. Researchers must be free to go to where their investigations take them; they are in the best positions to determine fruitful lines of enquiry and to pursue them. They may or may not be able to attract financial support for their work. They may be recruited as partners or consultants in particular research projects. But they must be free to decide whether they wish to be enlisted in these projects and to pursue their research without let or hindrance. Academic freedom, properly conceived, is part of accountability in that it supports the integrity of the teaching and research enterprise.

The second way in which accountability issues arise is with overbroad or loose claims of academic freedom. Recently one of Canada's multiversities initiated disciplinary action when one of its professors disclosed confidential information about a student for whom the professor had no teaching, supervisory, or administrative responsibility. Academic freedom was the defence claimed for this violation of confidentiality. Any experienced university person could offer additional examples of ill-conceived claims. There is in the ranks of the professoriate a libertarian view of academic freedom that accords immunity from the sanctions and consequences of bad behaviour. It is not a majority or even a prominent view, but it is present and sometimes asserted by faculty unions and others in answer to attempts to impose sanctions. The accountability problem here is that academic freedom is a core value of the academy, much like judicial independence is for the judiciary. Disagreement about its scope with consequent overbroad claims in its name undermines both understanding of and respect for this core value. Further, when there is disagreement within the academy on the meaning of academic freedom, how can we expect it to be legitimized and supported by external communities? Accountability of universities requires clarity and broad acceptance of the meaning of academic freedom.

In summary, there are reciprocal expectations that universities and governments have of one another. Universities expect governments to provide resources commensurate with the public good that they do. They also expect clarity and timely notice of government priorities and limitations, and respect for university governance and autonomy. In turn, governments expect or should expect responsiveness on mission, quality, and accountability. These expectations alone make for a close and vital relationship, but we can anticipate additional terms of engagement if multiversities emphasize their potential as institutions of democracy. This was the first priority in George Fallis's call for a renewed social contract between these institutions and the society they serve, and it is to this idea that we now turn.

Multiversities – which Fallis describes as "the distinctive adaptation of the university to the later twentieth century"[32] – have incurred two great liabilities: a weakened social contract and its concomitant mission drift. "Looking across all the characteristics of our age – across the constrained welfare state, the information technology revolution, post-modern thought, commercialization and globalization – and their implications for the multiversity, it is clear that something quite fundamental is changing. The character of our age threatens to transform the multiversity and its role in society. The multiversity is drifting, uncertain about the balance among its various tasks and ideals."[33]

To the historical role of universities in undergraduate, professional, and graduate education and research, and public service, is added "the idea of the multiversity as an institution of the economy, bringing together a new way of thinking about the university and a new way of thinking about the economy."[34] This added role threatens to overshadow the historical role and must be met by a new emphasis on purpose beyond the economic mission. For Fallis, undergraduate liberal education is part of that new emphasis. Recognition of universities as "integral institutions of liberal democracy"[35] is the other part.

In calling for this recognition of multiversities, Fallis is not urging greater democracy in their internal governance. Nor is he proposing an abandonment of elite standards in favour of egalitarianism or alignment

of the university with "progressive" causes. What he means in identifying the multiversity as an institution of democracy "is that to be a
democracy a country requires many institutions, and the list of required
institutions goes beyond the familiar political institutions of a constitution, universal suffrage, and regular elections. One example of an
additional institution is a free press ... Now the multiversity should be
regarded as such an additional institution – democracy requires multiversities that have an explicit mission to contribute to democratic life."[36]

Democratic roles are not new to universities. Accessible university
education; liberal undergraduate education; the training of professionals to pay attention to the public interest in addition to their own
and their clients' interests; the role of professors as public intellectuals;
the responsibility of universities to serve "as critic and conscience in
a democratic society,"[37] to generate new knowledge and to assess its
impact, all speak to past and present democratic obligations. But they
have been implicit and Fallis believes they should be made explicit.
He refers to Daniel Bell's observation in 1967 that if "the business firm
was the key institution of the past one hundred years, because of its
role in organizing production for the mass creation of products, the
university will become the central institution of the next one hundred
years because of its role as the new source of innovation and knowledge."[38] Its public support, increased power, and new centrality to
post-industrial life mean that its responsibilities to democracy "must
be articulated and the institution held accountable for how well it ful-
fills these tasks."[39]

Specifically, Fallis cites Robert Dahl's concern that traditional institutions of primary and secondary education, the media, political parties, and interest groups are insufficient to equip citizens for effective
political participation in an age of globalization, increased complexity
of issues, and the communications revolution. "The role for the multiversity is clear: it can enhance the older institutions and provide new
means for civic education, political participation, information, and
deliberation."[40] The university builds on what Amy Gutman described
as a responsibility of primary and secondary education to develop democratic character,[41] but the "fundamental democratic purpose of a university is protection against the tyranny of ideas. Control of the creation
of ideas – whether by a majority or minority – subverts democracy."[42]

"As institutional sanctuaries for free scholarly inquiry, universities
can help prevent such subversion. They can provide a realm where new
and unorthodox ideas are judged on their intellectual merits; where the

men and women who defend such ideas are not strangers but valuable members of the community. Universities thereby serve democracy as sanctuaries of non-repression."[43]

The implications of this idea of the university include the following:

- An undergraduate education is also a liberal education. Fallis proposes that each multiversity would develop a liberal education minor.
- "The multiversity must accept society's greater interest in applied science research and in technology transfer. These are perfectly legitimate requests of a democratic sponsor."[44]
- Social value is a criterion for funding research, not only in applied science, but in the social sciences too.
- University professors accept their responsibilities as public intellectuals.
- The new social contract between universities and society supports deliberative democracy as well as representative democracy.

George Fallis's study is important because it is an excellent contemporary account of the multiversity and the challenges it faces. It is important, too, because he offers clear and credible proposals to address those challenges. However one views the nature and content of his new social contract, one conclusion is inescapable: the relationship between multiversities and their public sponsors is undergoing fundamental change, and it is incumbent upon universities to lead that change in collaboration with leaders from their public sponsors. University-government relations take on new meaning and importance in this process, and there will be differences, depending on whether provincial, federal, or municipal governments, or two or all three of them, are at the table.

The dynamic relationships between universities and their public sponsors remind us that university relations with governments are shaped not only through bilateral connections that each institution has with them. We saw in chapter 1 that universities arrange themselves in groups according to their profiles and common interests. The U15 and ACCRU are joined by provincial and regional bodies, including the Council of Ontario Universities, the conférence des recteurs et des principaux des universités du Québec, the Association of Atlantic Universities, and the Research Universities Council of British Columbia. The national body is the Association of Universities and Colleges of Canada. Established in 1911 and based in Ottawa, AUCC is "a membership organization providing university presidents with a unified voice and a forum for collective action."[45]

Though ably led and staffed, AUCC has a mission that is more easily articulated than advanced. The differences among its ninety-seven members are vast, and they challenge the potential for unified voice and collective action. And with education a provincial responsibility, its voice is directed primarily to a federal government whose engagement in post-secondary education is limited. Research, financial assistance for students, and university education for Aboriginals are matters in which the federal government has authority, and it is to them that its conversations with AUCC are primarily directed.

Notwithstanding limitations imposed by diversity of membership and the division of constitutional powers in a federal state, AUCC has enjoyed recent success as a collective lobbying organization. Key to its achievement was the 1995–2004 presidency of Robert Giroux, who understood that frustration among the presidents of what then was the G10 group of universities (the country's leading research institutions) threatened its continued existence. The G10 was formed to encourage a federal government agenda in support of research and innovation, not one focused on preserving, restoring, or increasing a block transfer of funds to the provinces for distribution among their post-secondary institutions. The prominence of these universities, and their contributions of 50 per cent or more to AUCC's budgeted revenues, meant that AUCC had to come to terms with G10 or risk dissolution or continuance in a diminished, weakened state. It did so. Through the patient but persistent diplomacy of M Giroux, the research and innovation agenda was embraced by AUCC, though not without scepticism of many of its (non-G10) members, and the structure for membership fees was reformed to alleviate the disproportionate burden on G10 universities for AUCC's costs.

M Giroux and his successors have been well connected in the corridors of power, and they have been adept at negotiating differences among their members in order to present a coherent, ambitious agenda compatible with interests of the national government. Some U15 (former G10) leaders remain inclined to a path separate from AUCC, but the federal government's preference to deal with universities collectively means that AUCC is an essential participant in key policy discussions. If the organization did not exist today, Canadian universities would be obliged to create it anew. Internal tensions will continue because differences among its members remain, but their presidents should recognize that their voices are more likely to be heard from inside rather than out-side AUCC. In the words of former UBC president Martha Piper, "University presidents must realize that Canada is a complicated country, and there are pieces of the puzzle that make a federal initiative work. Those key pieces must be in place for success and they can be put in place only through collective advocacy. One institution acting alone cannot do it."[46] Dr Piper recounts what this meant in an outreach to Ottawa by UBC: "Early in my presidency I decided to make the rounds in Ottawa with UBC's deans and senior administrators. They were excited by the opportunity to present their special projects to the national govern-ment. I met with them before our departure. I instructed them to say nothing particular to UBC initiatives; they were to make the case for an agenda developed in common with other universities. I knew that if the agenda were adopted, UBC would be a major beneficiary – and it was. But I knew, too, that other universities would benefit and the case for support had to be advanced in our common interests."[47]

Dr Piper's words apply equally to provincial and regional bodies within Canada, and to international alliances of universities. Collabora-tion and partnerships[48] are more important than ever, and enlightened self-interest for their institutions will lead successful presidents to work towards common agendas among themselves and with other organiza-tions. Collective advocacy is not only desirable, it is essential.

Chapter Five

Grateful Dogs: On Philanthropy, Commercialization, and Partnerships

On a beautiful early autumn day in 2002, an outdoor crowd gathered on the grounds of the University of Saskatchewan's Western College of Veterinary Medicine. The opening of a magnetic resonance imaging (MRI) and radiation therapy centre for small animals was a notable event. Enhanced diagnostic and therapeutic services for companion animals offered treatment improvements, together with teaching and research opportunities that had attracted philanthropists and other supporters who were now present to be publicly named and thanked.

It is a duty of university presidents to say thank you on occasions such as this, and I arrived on the scene as the event preparations were concluding. In addition to invited guests and friends, organizers had arranged for the presence of a number of dogs – some bandaged – that were ostensibly grateful for their MRI-assisted care in the new centre. Also present to receive the guests of honour was a solitary player of the bagpipes, whose task it was to lead them to the site at which the formalities would take place. They soon arrived and joined the planned procession as the piper started his skirl. In response, a few of the dogs began to bark, and soon were joined by others in a cacophony of yelps, whimpers, and howls as the piper continued with determination. Overcome by laughter, I struggled to regain my composure for the official duties that were to follow. Fortunately, our guests of honour shared the amusement of others present for the event.

Fundraising has moved rapidly from the periphery of presidential lives closer to their centre. Though, in the past, Canadian university presidents were expected to be opportunistic in tapping private sources of wealth, it was not part of their job description until the last few decades. Some of the older universities had accumulated appreciable endowments – appreciable by modest Canadian standards – but more as a result of longevity than concerted effort. On becoming a dean of law twenty-five years ago, I realized that my university had no substantial, central fundraising capacity. When I sought advice and assistance in this area from the only university employee with fundraising in his job description, I was told that he "didn't do law." His efforts were limited to two of the university's thirteen colleges – engineering and agriculture – that had any history of private fundraising. So off to school I went and to a short course on philanthropy run by the Canadian Centre for Philanthropy, one of the two precursors of Imagine Canada.[1]

Now university presidents and deans can expect to be appraised, in part, on their success in fundraising. In this they are supported by departments of development or advancement, with senior leadership that typically includes professional fundraisers and often have under their umbrella university offices concerned with alumni, communications, and public relations. Universities mount ambitious campaigns and engage in ongoing fundraising, often with annual targets, that require much presidential time and commitment.

Among the reasons for this change is the fact that Canadian universities looked with envy upon fundraising success in universities and colleges in the United States – home to many of the finest postsecondary institutions in the world, where it was clear that the accumulation of large endowments was part of this success story. When public support for post-secondary education in Canada declined as health care trumped education in public policy and spending, the American example was even more compelling. With growing investment in fundraising capacity and a natural alumni support base, Canadian universities became more committed to attracting donations.

"The influence of the private economy on the university is undeniable. Wealthy donors clearly alter the shape of the institution through the power of their benefactions."[2] But their donations are courted and welcomed because their benefactions add value, and apart often from designating their general purpose, donors are usually content to defer to the university in the academic and related financial matters that determine the use of the donation. Provided that its purpose is one that is welcomed by the university, and that the donor is content to remain at arm's length from its related academic decision-making, a donation or gift is positive support for the institution and its students.

Every university president has had to say no to prospective donors. Sometimes a donation is offered for a purpose that cannot be entertained by the institution, because it is not part of the present or intended university mission and plans. Sometimes a donation is offered with strings attached that are inappropriate;[3] if the prospective donor cannot be persuaded to relent, it must be declined.

This does not mean that donors write cheques, receive thanks, and are not heard from again. On the contrary, successful fundraising depends on sustaining and growing donor interest, and this means nurturing the connections that inspire their generosity. One positive feature of university leadership is coming to know people with a lot of money who want to do something noble with it. Once enlisted to an excellent university purpose or project, they want to feel connected to it, to hear about successes or even setbacks, perhaps to offer their advice and encouragement, and often to provide additional financial support. They are justly proud of their efforts to make a positive difference, and there is ample scope for their being kept informed about and connected to activities supported by their donations without becoming involved in academic decision-making.

It is rare that donor relationships present difficult issues. Universities usually have well-established protocols that govern them, and donor expectations are typically compatible with these protocols. It is when the relationship extends beyond benefaction that it may raise questions about its alignment with university purpose, autonomy, or academic freedom. The commercialization of our universities – "efforts to sell the work of universities for a profit"[4] – is a prominent theme in contemporary debate on their current state and direction. Emblematic clothing, alumni tours, patented or patentable discoveries all may be for sale. Opportunities for others to profit may also be commercially available in the form of exclusive soft drink contracts or spaces for the display of corporate or commercial logos. Niche academic programs may cater to private interests – for a price. Even a research agenda can be agreed upon in contracts with external interests or in consultancies involving academic staff. These activities bring universities into the marketplace, and each presents them with difficult questions about how far they want to go, and for what price.

Universities have also entered the world of advertising. Most of them have engaged in branding in attempts to capture their most prominent features, achievements, or ambitions, and to bring them to the attention of their publics. They tout greatness more often than it is deserved and occasionally make claims of quality or impact that would leave a circus barker blushing with modesty. Catching the attention of prospective students, employees, partners, or commercial interests is important, and advertising helps universities to do so, but the line between advertising and puffery is a thin one, and it ill becomes them to cross it.

The roots of commercialization in American universities are explored by Derek Bok, who wrote that by the end of the twentieth century, universities were receiving growing attention and with it, new opportunities to make money. No longer were they "quiet enclaves removed from the busy world, they had emerged as the nation's chief source for the three ingredients most essential to continued growth and prosperity: highly trained specialists, expert knowledge, and scientific advances others could transform into valuable new products or life-saving treatments and cures."[5]

Bok observes that commercialization "has plainly taken root" in American higher education.[6] "What made commercialization so much more prevalent in American universities after 1980 was the rapid growth of opportunities to supply education, expert advice, and scientific knowledge in return for handsome sums of money."[7] Science had helped win the Second World War, thus earning heavy investment that yielded impressive results in defence, space exploration, electronics and computer technology, and biotechnology.[8] By the late decades of the twentieth century, an economic slowdown combined with the emergence of powerful new competitor nations shifted priority to the economy.[9] With passage of the 1980 Bayh-Dole Act,[10] subsidies to joint university-business ventures, and tax breaks encouraging industry to invest in university science, resulted in increased patents, royalties, licensing fees, and business-university collaborations. These, together with advances in genetics, resulted in a growth of the corporate share of university research from just over 2 per cent in the early 1970s to 8 per cent only thirty years later. In short, "a brave new world had emerged filled with attractive possibilities for turning specialized knowledge into money."[11] And it was a highly competitive new world, as the institutional rivalry that had always been present in American higher education intensified in the new environment.[12]

Commercialization is resisted by many who fear that business values and methods are anathema to the academy. They may overlook the possibility that universities can learn some things from the world of commerce: the importance of lowering costs and improving efficiency, the value of working continuously to improve quality, and the importance of timely adaptation to new circumstances.[13] But there are limits to what they can learn. Consumer demand may determine goods that are produced, but it is not a useful guide in curriculum development or identifying a research agenda. Well-known measures of business success are not matched by equivalents in "the more uncertain and ambiguous"[14] enterprise of a university. "In sum, the ways of the marketplace are neither consistently useful nor wholly irrelevant in trying to improve the performance of research universities. That is what makes the problem of commercialization difficult. Educators must use their own judgment in deciding when to pursue opportunities for profit or adopt other business practices."[15] But that judgment must be guided by sound policy and a sense of proportion about the extent to which for-profit activities are appropriate in institutions that have broader public purposes and responsibilities.

Bok examines three areas of concern in the United States: high-profile athletic programs, scientific research, and for-profit education, and considers lessons learned from each. The high-profile athletics programs reveal that "American universities, despite their lofty ideals, are not above sacrificing academic values … in order to make money,"[16] and that anticipated profits are illusory. "Still another lesson … is how the lure of money can gradually redefine and legitimate practices that were officially condemned generations before,"[17] and finally, "high-profile athletic programs reveal the limited power of university presidents to reclaim academic values once lucrative commercial practices have won a firm foothold."[18]

Lessons from the commercializing of scientific research are that "universities have paid a price for industry support through excessive secrecy, periodic exposés of financial conflict, and sometimes, corporate efforts to manipulate or suppress research results."[19] The lessons from for-profit education are variable. Executive and other customized programs see the university and corporate sponsor (if there is one) interested in the same thing – quality. Corporate sponsors for continuing medical education may threaten education when accompanied by promotion of the sponsors' products.[20] And the internet offers uncertain but potentially attractive prospects, including financial returns that can be used to improve the educational mission generally.[21]

Evaluating the risks and rewards of commercialization is difficult, because both are imprecise. But they are real. The reward is money, and money matters. "In higher education, the cards are stacked against an institution that lacks an established reputation and a lot of money."[22] We may recall the earlier discussion of path dependency and the difficulty of diverting an institution from an established path. That established path may be mediocrity, excellence, and everything in between. With money comes an ability to recruit the best scholars, attract the best students, offer the finest facilities. "In all these ways the strongest universities tend to perpetuate themselves almost automatically."[23]

The risks are that academic standards and values can be undermined and reputation be compromised. Bok warns universities to protect their procedures for the appointment and promotion of professors; to ensure that student admissions are based on academic criteria; and to ensure that all of their decisions are made "to further the interests of students and society rather than to please a powerful trustee, fit the private convenience of faculty, or achieve other extraneous goals."[24] Reputation can be compromised if commercialization overwhelms other institutional goals, values, and professional standards. "At a time when cynicism is so prevalent and the need for reliable information is so important, any damage to the reputation of universities and to the integrity and objectivity of their scholars, weakens not only the academy but the functioning of our democratic, self-governing society."[25]

A further problem is that the advantage of commercialization – money – may be more tangible and imminent while the risks are seen to be more remote. In consideration of particular proposals, this may result in a predisposition in favour of commercialization. The implication is that "analyzing commercial opportunities in the usual ad hoc way is virtually certain to result in a decay of basic principles."[26] Universities need to consider commercialization as a process and develop rules that are consistent with its mission and values, and that are both understood and enforced.[27] Closer ties between research and industry are inevitable, but universities must develop rules that address excessive secrecy for commercial reasons, disclosure and avoidance of conflicts of interest, and university investment in companies started by its own faculty.

For Jennifer Washburn,[28] the remedy for excessive commercialization lies not in university rules but in federal regulation. The reason, she argues, "is that in recent years, universities have proven unwilling or unable to address these concerns collectively themselves because of the ceaseless competition for better rankings, money, and prestige that pits each university against the others."[29] Washburn calls for regulation in four areas: "(1) the creation of independent third party licensing bodies ... that would assume control over university tech transfer and commercialization activities nationwide; (2) an amendment to the Bayh-Dole Act clarifying that the true intent of the legislation is to promote widespread use of taxpayer-financed research, not to maximize short-term profits; (3) new requirements that all federally funded university scholars comply with strict conflict-of-interest laws; and (4) the creation of a new federal agency to administer and monitor industry-sponsored clinical drug trials submitted to the Food and Drug Administration."[30]

There are important differences between the American and Canadian university worlds. High-profile – and big money – athletic programs do not exist on any scale in Canada, and the student-athlete model remains paramount in this country. For-profit education is less developed. And perhaps most significant, businesses in Canada are less inclined to invest in university research than in the United States; to our detriment, innovation is not a common feature of business plans of Canadian companies. But while the trend in Canada lags behind that in its southern neighbour, it is moving in the same direction and towards greater commercialization. In particular, corporate sponsorships are more common, and one example linked them directly to the classroom. In June 2013 it was reported that a study published in the *Journal of Medical Ethics* took issue with lectures given by a guest lecturer to second-year medical students at the University of Toronto. The lectures were on the subject of opioids – drugs used in pain management – and were reported to have been supported by pharmaceutical companies that market these drugs and given by a member of their speakers' bureau.[31] So in Canada, as in the United States, academic integrity requires protocols by which to assess commercial opportunities. Washburn's message portends external regulation in the absence of unwillingness or inability to develop them, and her warning should be taken as extending to Canada.

Although these protocols must be developed by universities themselves, it is possible to identify what should be common elements. The integrity of teaching and research is foremost among them, and its protection should rule out any commercial activity that intrudes or threatens intrusion upon the independence and professional standards by which students are taught and research is undertaken. This does not preclude contract teaching and research, but it does preclude prescription on matters affecting how the teaching and research will be done. In addition, protocols must contain policies on conflict of interest that prevent pecuniary or proprietary conflicts where possible, and require disclosure in any situation where they are present. To these we should add the protections suggested by Bok: protect procedures for the appointment and promotion of professors, and ensure that university admissions are based on academic criteria and that the interests of students and the public remain at the centre of university work.

A development in Canada that has attracted greater public attention than commercialization per se is partnerships among different institutions that seek to advance a common interest, or ones with joint university, government, and industry participation. Many of the questions that demand society's attention today require investigation on a scale and breadth that is beyond the capacity of solitary investigators or even small clusters of them. Larger multidisciplinary teams, often from different institutions, are involved, and the issues before them are of interest beyond the academy to government and industry whose engagement is required for the work to proceed. Their work is complex and expensive and must attract different partners to be achievable.

These partnerships can be difficult to assemble. There is a risk that each party may bring to them a myopia borne of its particular interests. Each is vulnerable to a proprietary view of the prospective enterprise. Universities want their work to be unfettered by external commitments, while governments are often focused on immediate and local issues, and on opportunities that can play out to their benefit now or soon. Industry can be prone to viewing research partnerships as the next best thing to an in-house research capacity. Successful partnership requires that boundaries be transcended and common interests be defined and pursued. And the partnership must be organized and governed in ways satisfactory to all.

Three Canadian examples of partnership will be considered here for their differences, not their similarities, and for the lessons they yield on best practices in developing partnerships. One is a university-industry-government partnership; a second is between a philanthropist and one university; and the third involves two universities and an independent think tank. The three partnerships are in their relatively early stages, so lessons learned from them are speculative rather than demonstrable. But if the premise underlying the present discussion is correct – that we shall see more of these partnerships – the experience of the present examples may be useful in developing those to come. For each of the three, the idea of partnership had origins in a compelling concept.

The importance of food security was the motivation for the first example. The earth's population is about two-and-a-half times what it was mere generations ago – from three billion to more than seven billion – and it is projected to reach nine billion by the middle of this century. Feeding a population of these numbers on a planet already under stress from present needs of its creatures on land and in the water is one of the great challenges before us. "Agricultural production needs to be substantially increased – by 60 percent – in the next four decades to meet the growing demand for food," according to the agricultural outlook for 2012–21 published by the OECD and the Food and Agricultural Organization of the United Nations.[32] The degradation of agricultural land and the effects of global warming may exacerbate the challenge, while the reduction of the one-third of production currently wasted may attenuate it.[33] Regardless, the imperative remains: agricultural production must grow substantially to avoid food shortage and starvation for growing numbers of the earth's population. These thoughts inspired reflection on Saskatchewan's responsibility and role in helping to meet the world's need for food security.

The province of 652,000 square kilometres, including 60,000 square kilometres of water, is home to only 1.1 million people. Two of its lakes – Athabasca and Reindeer – cover areas larger than Canada's smallest province of Prince Edward Island. It has more than 40 per cent of Canada's arable land and is part of the Great Plains agricultural region. Its provincial university counts among its strengths agriculture and related disciplines and is home to an impressive cluster of university, government, and commercial facilities on a campus that includes one of Canada's most successful innovation parks.[34] Also based in the province is Potash Corporation of Saskatchewan – a leading food company – the world's largest producer of potash and fertilizer.

The responsibility – and the opportunity – were manifest and led me to host Premier Wall and PotashCorp president Bill Doyle for lunch at my on-campus home early in 2011. We discussed the issues of food security and agreed that Saskatchewan had a duty to lead in addressing them. The province, the university, and the corporation – in combination – possessed formidable and unique capacity to undertake this role. Thus was born the idea of the Global Institute for Food Security (GIFS), with initial financial commitments of $35 million from PotashCorp and $15 million from the provincial government.

Commitments on this scale do not come in the expectation that it is the responsibility of government and corporation to write cheques and the duty of the university to define, develop, and launch the institute as it sees fit. The parties have continuing interests and accountabilities – government to its citizens, corporation to its shareholders, and university to its several communities – that require their ongoing engagement as partners in the project. But what kind of partnership would it be?

The task of translating the concept into substance fell to senior leaders in the three organizations, and they began the necessary conversation. Wayne Brownlee, PotashCorp executive vice-president and treasurer, was critical of what he saw as the usual expectations of universities: "Too often in the past universities approached potential corporate donors saying, in effect, 'Here is our expertise and we want you to fund it.' A better approach is a business development model focusing on the needs of prospective supporters and linking needs to expertise within the university."[35] He felt that universities require business development officers in addition to people soliciting gifts. The Global Institute for Food Security was, however, a natural project from the beginning. "It just came together and I can't remember a time when we [PotashCorp] had a fundamental disagreement."[36] He reported some concern between the university and government, but "never did I think that we were not going to establish the institute," said Brownlee, "and we insisted that it had to be a tripartite arrangement – university, PotashCorp, and government – or it would not happen."[37]

For the province's deputy minister of agriculture Alanna Koch, the hurdles in the way of a tripartite partnership were significant. "Each party brings its own challenges and organizational peculiarities. For government, translating and communicating the original idea and concept to ministers and the public service is not easy, particularly with an election intervening as talks were getting underway."[38] But if governments have their organizational challenges, so do universities. "They can be territorial, rigid and inflexible. They can declare themselves open to partnerships, but their structures and cultures do not easily accommodate them. Governments and companies need clear understandings on focus and measurable results in order to be accountable to the public and shareholders, and they need universities to understand this."[39] But all three need to be successful here; the leveraging that partnerships like this brings will be more common and important because "public dollars are not available in the same ways they have been."[40]

For the University of Saskatchewan the key issues were the mission of the proposed centre (a global institute, not a provincial one) and assurances of the necessary independence in conducting research. The preferred model was inspired by the Canada Excellence Research Chairs program: recruit a world-leading scholar in food science and policy, and develop the capacity around him or her to build a pre-eminent program in global food quality and security.

Differences among the parties played out in discussions about structure. Should the new institute be a university centre, or should it be a separate organization? The case for the former included the university's formidable capacity in agriculture and veterinary medicine; its excellent Crop Development Centre; its robust connections with related federal and provincial agencies; and its infrastructure on campus. The case for the latter was rooted in anxiety about whether the institute could meet the needs of government and corporation if it was embedded in university structures and constrained by its rules, regulations, and culture. There was also concern that a university centre would be less adaptable to change as time went by, and in particular to bringing additional partners into its organization and activities.

The conversation among the three partners was assisted by the retention of global consulting firm McKinsey & Company. The consultant was central in identifying the potential role for Saskatchewan in addressing the food security challenge; the key elements of a collaborative research organization including governance, organizational structure, and policies; an operating model and funding strategy; and an implementation plan.

GIFS was established as a University of Saskatchewan type B centre, which, in the lexicon of centre models, has broad scope. It has its own board of directors with representatives from the three partners and it reports through the university's president to the board of governors. Its founding director and CEO, Dr Roger Beachy, was founder of the Danforth Plant Science Center in Missouri, first director of the National Institute of Food and Agriculture, and chief scientist of the United States Department of Agriculture. The governance framework includes an International Science Leadership Panel to consist of internationally recognized scientists to advise the director and board on international scientific trends; emerging research opportunities and challenges; knowledge translation; potential national and international collaborations and linkages; and principles and criteria for program proposals and adjudication. Research will be subject to the university's principles and policies pertaining to academic freedom.

GIFS is in its infancy and its success remains to be seen, but the feature of its early development that merits attention was the decision to retain McKinsey & Company to assist in developing the institute. Global consultants have resources that are not found in-house in universities, companies, and governments, and they are well placed to assist all three in transcending institutional interests, in advising on best practices, and in developing an organizational model.

A second example is that of a philanthropist and one university. The Clayton H. Riddell Graduate Program in Political Management (GPPM) at Carleton University had its origins in the roles played by political staff in government. "As political staff to cabinet ministers and elected representatives, strategists and tacticians for political parties, campaign managers and communication officers, policy advocates for civil society organizations and grassroots movements, they are essential to democratic practice and to the institutions and apparatus of contested politics."[41]

Anyone experienced in dealing with governments has encountered scores of these "staffers." They are often the young people sitting quietly at the table in meetings with Cabinet ministers, or members of the advance teams that herald the imminent arrival of a senior elected politician. They connect, enquire, prepare, plan, follow up, counsel, and warn in the names of their principals. Their authority is derivative, but many of them become very influential, and they contribute to the successes or the failures of the politicians for whom they toil.

Political staff often bring little more than political commitment and enthusiasm to their work in the complicated environment of Parliament Hill, a provincial legislature, or city hall. It was the gap between their preparation and their important work that inspired the creation of the Carleton program, unique in Canada, in applied politics. The national capital was an ideal site: proximity to government, and to the people who gravitate to government, meant that resources already were at hand.

The program was made possible by a commitment of Calgary businessman and philanthropist Clayton Riddell to a $15 million donation to Carleton, and in May 2010 the parties signed a donor agreement. Among its provisions was one requiring the establishment, in accordance with university protocols, of a five-person program steering committee, with two members representing the Riddell Family Charitable Foundation (RFCF), two members representing Carleton University (CU), and a chair to be selected by mutual agreement between RFCF and CU (Preston Manning.) The purposes of the steering committee were set out in section 14 of the donor agreement:

a) To support the GPPM in implementing the GPPM proposal in Appendix A;
b) To ensure that the GPPM exposes students to the partisan nature of the political environment from a "cross-partisan perspective."
c) To advise the GPPM on strategic issues, such as curriculum development, program promotion and securing additional funding to ensure its long-term success;
d) To approve the annual budget, the selection of adjunct faculty and staff, including the Executive Director and to participate in the faculty hiring decisions;
e) To recommend to the Dean of Graduate Studies and Research Office regarding the awarding of the GPPM Scholarship and Bursary Fund described in Clause 5(b).
f) To prepare an annual report to the RFCF on the progress and performance of the GPPM.[42]

Appendix A referred to in 14(a) asserts that the program is to be a one-year, full-time master's degree: "Curriculum will reflect a practically-oriented professional degree"[43] and include required courses, a ten-week internship, and elective courses. Three required courses and six elective courses are then set out. While courses in ethics are not prescribed, it is intended that "ethics will be woven into the content of the degree at every turn as a governing concern."[44]

The program was announced and launched in 2010, and in 2011 the Canadian Press requested a copy of the donor agreement. Carleton refused, citing privacy concerns. The freedom of information commissioner ordered mediation, and Carleton released a redacted copy of the agreement in March 2012. The commissioner ordered Carleton to provide more information, and in June, the full text of the agreement was released. Protests from Carleton faculty and the Canadian Association of University Teachers (CAUT) quickly followed, and a *Globe and Mail* editorial observed, "Few would deny that a donor to a university should have some say in the conditions of his gift. But whatever its financial distress, a publicly funded university can't abandon or delegate its authority on matters of curriculum, staff and faculty hires, annual budgets and other responsibilities."[45]

On 24 July the university's president, provost, and dean of public affairs wrote to the university community, conceding that "the current wording of the section of the agreement relating to the role of the Steering Committee is open to misunderstanding and needs clarification" and promised a review to clarify the language.[46] The revised clause 14 stipulates that the program steering committee "will operate in accordance with all CU policies, procedures and practices" and amends section 14, clauses c, d, and e as follows:

c) To provide timely and strategic advice on program-related matters, including program direction, curriculum development, academic and administrative staffing, organization and promotion, and securing additional funding, to ensure the GPPM's long-term success.
d) To approve the annual budget disbursing the funds provided by the donor to the GPPM ensuring that it is aligned with the original proposal and/or mutually agreed-upon changes.
e) To advise the Dean of the Faculty of Graduate and Postdoctoral Affairs on policies governing awards from the GPPM Scholarship and Bursary Fund.

The amendments are substantial, in that section 14 must be read as subject to Carleton's policies, procedures, and practices, and clauses c and e are more specific on the steering committee's advisory role. The requirement of budgetary approval in clause d applies only to ensuring that funds provided by the donor are spent as agreed. Whether the changes will be sufficient to satisfy critics remains to be seen, though two lessons can be taken from what has transpired to date.

The first is that donor agreements should be drawn so that they can be made public in their entirety. Nothing in the original agreement justified a refusal to disclose it on privacy grounds. Had the agreement been public from the outset, the concerns that were raised could have been addressed in a timely fashion and without publicity that embarrassed the university and perhaps the donor.

Second, donors or their agents are entitled to give all the advice they want, whether informally or in structured processes. And universities are wise to hear their advice and to take it seriously. But the boundaries between advice and decision in academic matters must be clear. Carleton's administration responded to criticisms in ways suggesting that the boundaries were respected, even if they were not clear, and that may be the case. But the original agreement was not clear, with the result that an excellent initiative was launched amidst unfortunate and preventable controversy.

The third example of an institutional partnership is the Balsillie School of International Affairs (BSIA) in Waterloo, Ontario. The school was founded in 2007 by three equal partners, one a think tank and two universities: the Centre for International Governance Innovation (CIGI), the University of Waterloo, and Wilfrid Laurier University. Its declared vision is to be a hub of a global network of scholars, practitioners, and students coming together "to develop new solutions to humanity's critical problems, improve global governance now and in the future, and enhance the quality of people's lives around the world."[47]

Preparing the governance document for the school was, in the view of Balsillie Chair of Global Systems Thomas Homer-Dixon, "an enormously stressful and contentious project,"[48] in part because of the early departures of two of the school's previous directors, and a CAUT report that was highly critical of the circumstances in which one of them was dismissed.[49] Homer-Dixon was charged with leading the governance project, and he described CIGI as "very constructive" in the task.[50] "This was not a case of CIGI on one side and universities on the other." CIGI president Rohinton Medhora agreed: "CIGI was often the salami in the sandwich between the aspirations of two universities with distinct cultures and goals."[51] Preparation of the governance document for the school proved an arduous task over eighteen months. The result is a comprehensive governance blueprint including detailed annexes that constitute a useful model for development of other partnerships. "The governance document states that the three partners bring to BSIA different but complementary strengths, so they have different roles and responsibilities. The two universities employ BSIA faculty and offer BSIA's academic programs. CIGI, as a think tank, uses its in-house expertise and its worldwide network of practitioners to help inform and guide BSIA's outreach and collaborative research."[52]

BSIA is separately incorporated, with a board of six directors, two from each partner, including a senior administrator from each of the universities and CIGI, a faculty member from each of Waterloo and Laurier, and an additional CIGI representative. The board oversees BSIA management and has final budgetary and operational authority.[53] A director, appointed to lead BSIA,[54] chairs a management team, which includes an associate director from each of the universities and a CIGI representative. The management team "oversees the operation of BSIA's major activities and facilitates synergies among them." There is also a council consisting of all BSIA faculty, the management team, two staff members, and two students to provide a forum for discussion and recommendations "about any and all matters of interest to BSIA."[55]

The challenge in a collaborative initiative such as this is to develop cohesiveness so that the school has collective identity and purpose and is not simply a facility to which faculty have recourse from their home institutions as they deem useful to them. The sum of a partnership must be greater than its parts, or why have the partnership at all? The key to collective identity is the position of director, who must be empowered to do more than broker partner interests; he must have authority to ensure that Balsillie School members are committed to the institution. The detailed governance documents should assist in this task. Of note in this respect is Annex G, sections 3[56] and 4(6),[57] which together give the director of BSIA significant influence. Section 3 sets out in considerable detail the roles and responsibilities of senior faculty in the Balsillie School, and section 4(6) provides that, upon appointment or renewal of BSIA senior faculty by either Waterloo or Laurier, the BSIA director shall be invited to provide a written assessment of the candidates' qualifications and fulfilment of Balsillie School responsibilities. These are important, because they make clear that the director has a substantive role in assigning Balsillie School duties and ensuring that they are carried out. Written input by the director into performance reviews should help to build the collective identity and purpose sought by the school.

Another important provision in developing the school's identity is Annex E,[58] which allows the director to appoint BSIA fellows and external scholars. Given the school's mission on global governance, it is essential that it have the authority and opportunity to invite outstanding scholars from anywhere in the world to join its ranks for collaborative research projects.

The Balsillie School and the partnership it represented did not escape the attention of the Canadian Association of University Teachers. Labelling CIGI as "Jim Balsillie's private think tank,"[59] its delegates in spring 2012 passed a motion "that unless the two universities change the governance structure for the Balsillie School of International Affairs so that academic integrity is ensured, censure will be imposed on the administrations of those two universities."[60] CAUT censure is of no legal force, but no one welcomes denunciation by a national organization, and so the issue of censure was joined by Waterloo and Laurier universities.

The Canadian Association of University Teachers did not approach censure without context; it had its own views of collaboration and partnerships. In April 2012 it published its Guiding Principles for University Collaborations.[61] The first principle addresses the protection of academic freedom, which, apart from definitional concerns discussed in the previous chapter, is not controversial. The second principle deals with academic integrity, which is not defined at all, though we are told in the accompanying narrative that "the protection of academic integrity involves more than protection against direct intrusion on the academic freedom of the researchers and the autonomy of the university … Integrity can also be compromised by indirect distortion of the core academic relationships and functions of universities and their faculty. It is very important that various aspects of academic relationships within the university not be inappropriately influenced by donor or other collaborative research arrangements. Nor should the overall work of the university and its units be distorted by such agreements."[62]

Without a definition of academic integrity distinct from academic freedom and institutional autonomy, it is difficult to determine the meaning and reach of these words. Arguably they could be interpreted to preclude change in the ways the university goes about its business. One can imagine debates on the subject, the course of which might depend on whether the speaker liked the prospective partner or was among the beneficiaries of the proposed arrangement. This prospect is not remote in view of other provisions in the CAUT document (numbered here for reference below):

1. Academic staff shall play the central role in decisions regarding the initiation, development, implementation, monitoring, and assessment of donor and other collaborative agreements.[63]
2. Donor and other collaborative agreements should be governed by a committee at least two-thirds of whom are elected academic staff members who do not hold administrative positions.[64]
3. In no case should a funder or a private collaborator or representative have any voice in matters related to the academic affairs of the institute or academic aspects of the collaboration.[65]

I will address the potential impacts of these provisions below, but for immediate purposes it is sufficient to note that CAUT approaches the ideas of collaboration and partnership with deep reservations. The senates of both Waterloo and Laurier approved the governance document for the Balsillie School, but that was not enough for CAUT. Its principles document declares that "there are occasions in which collegial governance structures can be corrupted,"[66] and intervention by the association may be required, and presumably this was such an occasion. Precisely what this means for university autonomy is not explored in the document.

Thomas Homer-Dixon took the lead in responding to the CAUT threat of censorship. "When it comes to academic freedom in Canada," he said, "CAUT has made itself the legislator, police, prosecutor, judge, jury and executioner all rolled into one."[67] To CAUT president Jim Turk's description of CIGI as "Balsillie's private think tank,"[68] Homer-Dixon referred to CIGI's status as a public charitable organization and described its funding sources, including $30 million from the Government of Canada and $17 million from the province. He also described its governance arrangements, which include an operating board with experts from public and private sectors as well as an international board of governors. Balsillie chairs the operating board and does not sit on the international board of directors.

To CAUT's charge that Balsillie or his "private charity" has voice in Balsillie's academic affairs,[69] Homer-Dixon replied in an open letter to CAUT President Turk that BSIA has two components: academic programs and a research institute. Academic programs are mounted and staffed by Waterloo and Laurier faculty; the two universities and CIGI participate together in the administration of the research institute. He pointed out that the distinction has long been a matter of public record and criticized CAUT for its "systematic misrepresentation" of the governance document.

The threat of censure did not end quickly. In September 2012, Laurier and Waterloo hosted a conference on academic freedom in hopes it would clarify differences, and in particular compel CAUT to specify what it meant by shifting the basis for its critique from academic freedom to academic integrity. A month later, the two universities and CIGI completed a memorandum of understanding in which they "elaborate certain of the principles set forth in the Governance Document"[70] previously approved by the three parties. Its terms are carefully drawn to emphasize university prerogatives in the partnership,[71] though it appears to be a face-saving device to allow the disputants to reconsider their paths. CAUT pronounced itself well satisfied with the result and withdrew its consideration of censure, even though the MOU did not amend or qualify the Balsillie School Governance Document that had precipitated the dispute. In the words of University of Waterloo professor and CIGI chair Thomas Homer-Dixon, "The whole thing was completely unnecessary, involved an enormous amount of emotional trauma on all sides and, frankly, the governance document that we designed ... stands exactly intact, word for word."[72]

We should now consider the potential impact of the CAUT guidelines numbered above. Guidelines 1 and 2 can be criticized on four grounds. First, they have the potential to violate the academic freedom of some faculty; second they would vest academic staff with authority over matters for which they are not responsible, thereby sidelining administrative personnel and governance bodies whose responsibility it is to develop and oversee partnerships; third, they propose an unpredictable process for approval that would discourage collaboration and lead to more private sector collaboration through consultancies rather than partnerships; and fourth, these guidelines would discourage philanthropy.

Underlying the first criticism is the idea that if we can conceive of academic freedom being owned, it is owned by individuals – the members of the academic staff. And in important respects it is both sword and shield. Properly conceived as outlined earlier,[73] it is both freedom to teach and conduct research, and protection against recrimination or sanction for its exercise. For many faculty the exercise of academic freedom includes engagement with others from outside the academy as well as from within. We need only think of the crop scientist developing new crop varieties in collaboration with primary producers, cooperatives, agribusiness, or government departments of agriculture; or the engineer whose interest in material science leads her to collaborate with an aircraft manufacturer in developing lighter, stronger components for aircraft manufacture. Their work may require partnerships for financial and other reasons, and subjecting their ability to form partnerships to approval of an elected faculty committee could impede it, and thereby their academic freedom.

The second criticism rests on the well-known proposition that responsibility should abide with authority. University administrations are responsible for developing partnerships leading to investment and philanthropic support that will advance the university's mission and increase its capacity to do its work well. Academic matters affected by this work are subject to the approval of senates or equivalent bodies, while financial questions are referable to boards of governors. And it is the president who is answerable to the board and university communities for strengthening the university's fundraising capacity, and for securing resources from this and other sources. The idea that academic

staff have the central role in this area is at variance with these responsibilities. And the further idea that donor and collaborative agreements
should be governed by elected faculty committees is a bad one for three
reasons: first, it would intrude on the governance responsibilities of
boards and senates; second, it would vest authority over donor agreements in an elected faculty committee while responsibility for securing resources lies elsewhere; and third, an elected faculty committee
would leave the university with the luck of the draw (electoral process)
in terms of the qualities required for this work.

The third criticism arises from both tone and substance of the CAUT
guidelines. The tone is one of grudging acceptance of university partnerships, accompanied by a pervasive suspicion that university administrators will compromise academic protocols and values in their endless quests for money. Faced with these guidelines, and in particular
with elected faculty governance of collaborations, many prospective
collaborators would eschew partnerships and rely instead on consultancies in which the faculty member is hired on a contract for services.
Such consultancies have their advantages for industry and government
needing the academy's expertise. They are simple, fast, and more easily concluded on their terms. The external body gets what it wants; the
faculty member receives financial reward; the university gets little or
nothing. In contrast, partnerships typically engage a broader participation with opportunities and benefits more widely distributed within
the university.

Fourth, these guidelines would discourage philanthropic donations to universities. Donors want their financial contributions to be
welcomed and appreciated. They do not want them to be grudgingly
accepted and subject to approval requirements that bypass governing bodies and administration in favour of elected faculty members
who would not be accountable for the quality of their decisions on
donor and collaborative agreements. "Thank you very much," potential donors would say, "I'll take my money elsewhere," to the great
detriment of our universities.

We should reflect, too, upon guideline 3 precluding funders, collaborators, or their representatives from having any voice in academic
matters. Are we so jealous and protective of academic matters that we
must deny collaborators any voice in them? Are they of such delicacy
that we must erect fences around them to protect them from outsiders
presumably bent on displacing or unduly influencing academic decision-makers? Do they demand expertise to which no outsider can be

expected to add value? The purity sought by CAUT in denying any voice to outsiders in these matters would come at a very high price.

Finally, we can summarize lessons yielded by the Balsillie School example for those seeking to build partnerships. The most important is the necessity to address governance at the outset. The Balsillie School experienced early difficulties, including departures of two directors prior to the development of a comprehensive blueprint and set of annexes that should stabilize the school and serve as a template for others engaged in developing partnerships of this kind.

Also important is the need to ensure that an entity borne of the partnership is greater than the sum of its parts, that it is not a shell or simply a nice facility that provides convenient recourse to scholars from responsibilities in their home units. This is the institutional cohesiveness to which Homer-Dixon referred, and it is achieved by requiring committed participation in the new entity's mission and program. This means that the leader of the new school must have real authority, which the director of the Balsillie School should have through his participation in recruitment and annual reviews of personnel in the two universities who are also associated with the school.

Academic freedom was guaranteed in the process of developing the Balsillie School, but it is essential to be prepared to demonstrate that this is so in order to head off or meet controversy on the subject. As for the controversy itself, it is important to be clear about its nature. At its heart were different understandings about the role of universities in our society. The Canadian Association of University Teachers has its feet firmly planted in the past on this subject. Anchoring its critique in an undefined concept of academic integrity, its concern about preventing distortion of core academic relationships and functions masks a suspicion of change to the ways in which universities go about their business, including embarking on new organizational ventures that partnership may bring. It is to be hoped that CAUT will see the Balsillie School example as containing lessons for itself, as it does for the rest of us.

In summary, Canadian universities can anticipate more opportunities for partnerships comparable to the above examples. The costs of exploring big issues are high – in most cases, more than can be met by unrestricted donations, or assembled by single entities, whether universities, governments, or businesses. These entities must become more comfortable with the idea of partnerships and more adept at developing them. In particular, universities must have or develop protocols, not only on donations and commercial activities, but on partnerships. Those applicable to the first two will have some application to partnerships, particularly as they relate to teaching and research. But as the examples demonstrate, governance and transparency must be addressed early in their development, and external assistance may be helpful in bringing the parties together under terms and conditions that meet the needs of all.

Chapter Six

Let's Make a Deal: On Governance, Collegial Management, and Collective Bargaining

It was February in the university's centennial year of 2007 and I was out of the country but had reached the provost by phone. He was on his way into Deans' Council and wanted to know what message I had for the deans on the immediate prospect of a faculty strike. Collective bargaining had become protracted, and the faculty union had an ambitious agenda that included workloads, faculty complement, and representation on the board of governors. In addition, I knew that the union leadership was ill-disposed towards the direction of the university in recent years. It was prepared to utilize negotiations and possible job action as a vehicle through which to express opposition, in anticipation that it might destabilize the institution and force change, in direction and possibly university leadership.

I said to the provost that he could report to the deans that I shared their concerns about the prospects for a strike. I had lived through them and was familiar with the tension and rancour they bring, and the damage they can do. But there were worse things, I said, and I was not prepared to see lasting damage caused to the university by bargaining on the matters on the union's agenda. I asked the provost to inform the deans that I would never authorize negotiations on workload, faculty complement, and governance, and if a strike was the price to be paid, it was unavoidable.

Despite differences in size, mission, resources, and quality, there are organizational similarities among universities that attest to their common origins, and in particular the idea that universities are communities that govern themselves. The architecture of self-government typically includes separate bodies empowered by statute, charter, or other authority to address academic and financial matters.[1] Nomenclature varies, but in Canada, senate and board of governors are common names for these bodies and will be used here.

There are sound reasons for this division of powers. Senates are made up of members of the academic community – faculty, students, and academic administration – and have plenary authority for establishing and supervising academic programs and activities. Ranging in size from twenty-five members to more than two hundred, with an average of seventy-six,[2] these are people who are familiar with universities as academic communities and who are prepared to commit time and effort to their governance, and they are appropriately entrusted with their academic oversight. Boards of governors are empowered to supervise and decide on university finances, business, and property, and their membership includes (or should include) members who can bring the requisite expertise and experience to the table.

These separate spheres of activity are not watertight compartments. Senate deliberations may necessarily be influenced by financial matters, which may lead it or its committees to comment and advise on them. Board deliberations on budget must be informed by an understanding of the university's strategic plan and academic priorities, which make it a participant in planning activities. This overlap of interests means that bicameralism is not inevitable. In 1972 the University of Toronto replaced its senate and board of governors with a new unicameral governing council, but it is one of the few Canadian institutions to have adopted this model. Others live with the overlap that is resolved in contentious matters by focusing on authority to decide.

The composition of senates is less controversial than is that of boards. The latter have ranged in size among different universities from eleven to more than sixty members[3] who are ex officio, or who have been elected or appointed by different bodies. In addition to external members, they typically include faculty, students, and sometimes others, including union representatives. Individual conflicts of interest are common, and so is the potential that such boards will behave more as constituent assemblies than governing bodies. This is a problem for universities, and it is a problem for governments, whether they recognize it or not. Self-governance is possible in public institutions only if its mechanisms and behaviours are compatible with sound governance principles that adequately protect the public interest. This means that all board members have fiduciary responsibility for the best interests of the university as a whole. Boards of governors that have too many insiders, or whose insiders behave like delegates from bodies that elect or appoint them, fail to discharge this responsibility.

Boards should have a significant majority of members from outside the university. These are the independent members, and their majoritarian presence is needed to ensure that the financial matters with which boards are primarily concerned are addressed in ways free of conflict of interest and in the name of the public, as distinct from internal university constituencies. Of course, it is essential that these public members be appointed because they have backgrounds that qualify them for the job. Oversight of finances in the hundreds of millions and sometimes billions of dollars in university operating and capital budgets is part of the job. The appointment of the university's president is another. These are responsibilities that require people with backgrounds to ask the right questions of the university's senior executives and who understand the qualities required to lead universities. Too often these are not the people appointed. Prior to 2000 at the University of Saskatchewan, for example, public representatives on the board of governors were appointed more because of their affiliation with the governing party and less on account of their qualifications, and this was so regardless of the party in power. There were exceptions, of course, and sometimes those appointed because of their political affiliation became excellent board members, but they were exceptions that proved the rule. People who are appointed because of their politics rather than their qualifications too often see themselves as representing concerns other than the best interests of the university. And because they are not qualified for the demanding tasks of board oversight, they are prone to focus their attention elsewhere, leading to micromanagement in matters that should not command their attention.

In 1999, the University of Saskatchewan petitioned the government to bring an end to board appointment practices that had been so detrimental to governance, and the province's two universities signed a protocol with the government that led to a marked improvement in the qualifications of those named to the board. The protocol called for regular consultation on government appointments and required eligible names to be approved by both government and university. Retired Bank of Canada president Gordon Thiessen was the first appointment under the protocol, and his selection set a high standard for the new process, a standard that on the whole has been sustained in the years since the protocol was signed.

University employees as well as the general public often are unaware of the extraordinary public service contributions of external board members. These are not corporate boards they sit on, with annual compensation in the many thousands of dollars. University board members are either not paid or the recipients of a modest expense per diem that can only be described as token. They are often professionals whose board duties take them from law and accounting firms, other professional offices, and businesses. The annual time commitment of board members may be thirty days a year, and many more for board and committee chairs. They serve because they are often graduates of the university or otherwise connected to it, and they care deeply about its welfare. They deserve the profound gratitude of the university communities they serve, and the public in whose name they act.

And now we turn our attention again to senates, which, to be effective, must have excellent and efficient committees, regular meetings with president and provost present, and timely information about the state and current circumstances of the university. Most senate work will be conducted by committees reporting to the plenary body that must approve their plans and proposals. If committees do their work well, meetings of the whole should be efficient and reserved for discussions of the most important issues, whether in committee recommendations or the reports of the president and provost. These senior executives must be present for the great majority of senate meetings. Universities have internal accountabilities as well as external ones, and the participation of president and provost in senate, presenting their reports, participating in debate, and responding to questions of members in public meetings is an important component of internal accountability. And timely information is critical for these bodies if they are to engage in evidence-based decision-making. They must know how their university is faring relative to its peer institutions, and they should be well briefed on its current issues and circumstances.

The chair of the senate should be a faculty member elected by the body. Practice varies, with presidents or provosts serving in the chair at some universities. This has two negative features: one, a senior member of the executive serving in the chair is under constraints when participating in debates when he should be free to speak as the occasion demands; and two, a senate chaired by a member chosen by colleagues is more compatible with the accountability of president and provost to this senior academic body.

In their 2012 study of academic senates and university governance,[4] Pennock et al. asked university secretaries to identify key issues and challenges in their senates. Three themes stood out in the responses that are of concern here: "tension between the roles and responsibilities of the senate in relation to the university administration and board within university governance … issues and challenges associated with the tension between individual and constituency interests versus the interests of the university as a whole … [and] the challenge of engaging senate members."[5] The study further reported that "there is a gap between the roles that senate does play within the university and the role that it should play"[6] and that "the role and responsibilities of the senate need to be clarified."[7]

In addition to central university governance by senate and board of governors, there are mechanisms of collegial management within units of the university. Faculties, colleges, schools, and departments have their own councils, committees, and individuals with administrative authority over matters particular to these units. While the extent of that authority varies, depending on the institution, it is considerable in all of them. Upon becoming a dean in my university a quarter century ago, I was informed by the vice-president academic that central administration asserted little influence or direction, and that most of the decisions that mattered were made in colleges and departments. In effect, the university was a loose federation with decentralized authority concentrated in individual academic units.

Of course some matters are appropriately determined at local levels. In general they draw upon particular academic expertise of faculty at those levels. Curriculum and student assessment are the main ones, as they require relevant disciplinary knowledge. In addition, collegial management takes on other duties in the interest of efficient direction of local affairs. Assignments of duties, helping to shape timetables, and establishing and disestablishing departmental or faculty committees are all matters to be addressed locally, and if the unit head is wise, in transparent consultation with faculty.

The juxtaposition of university governance and collegial management raises several issues, including the determination of where local authority should begin and end, the roles of unit deans and heads in relation both to their units and central administration, the extent of administrative burdens that rest on the shoulders of individual faculty members, and the problem of multiple identities.

Identifying the limits of local authority is critically important. Some voices in our universities assert that all or most authority emanates from the bottom up. Precisely what this means in a particular context may not be clear, but it conjures up an image of collegial sentiment percolating amidst the rank and file of faculty, coalescing and slowly rising to envelop and instruct heads, deans, and the university's administration. The underlying concept is the maximizing of decision-making at the department level and its sharp curtailment beyond. This includes not only the matters mentioned above, but also some personnel decisions: hiring, awarding tenure, and promoting (note, not disciplining). This view concedes some authority beyond the unit, but not much. It ignores or plays down roles for individuals or bodies outside the department that may affect its plans and activities.

The problem is that the bottom-up view is incomplete and simplistic, the former because law and sound administrative practice recognize that how the unit goes about its work is not of interest only to the unit itself, the latter because it ignores the broader dispersal of authority in the university-wide context, including substantial statutory or other public authority given to deans and presidents. The problem is particularly acute in weak academic units, where the bottom-up view holds that people from outside these units can do little to address shortcomings. But the unit is weak largely because of what its members are doing, or perhaps not doing. Weak academic departments tend to perpetuate themselves because of their reluctance to apply standards higher than they see reflected in themselves. It is for this reason that engagement by deans and provosts may be needed.

The second issue presented by the juxtaposition of university governance and collegial management is the role of unit leaders, particularly the heads of academic departments within a faculty or college. One of the joys of decanal leadership – particularly in smaller units – is that the dean is present in the faculty, teaching its students and otherwise participating in its academic activities. It is inevitable that the dean is seen by colleagues and students as their champion in securing resources and otherwise representing the unit's interests in the wider university context. This holds true of department heads as well.

But university administrations have expectations too. Deans expect, or should expect, that heads are leading their departments in ways that conform to university and disciplinary standards of quality and effectiveness. Provosts and presidents expect similar things of deans in the wider context in which they work. This creates a necessary tension in which a dean or department head might be heard to say, "I have faculty on one side of me and the university administration on the other, and I can't satisfy both." The tension is more acute with department heads, whose daily lives unfold side-by-side with their faculty colleagues and students. And it is particularly acute in unionized environments where department heads are union members. Sometimes they are informally (and inappropriately) compared to shop stewards, a union office that emphasizes the protection of rights and the representation of members, not an important office of academic leadership responsible for high academic standards of scholarship in teaching and research.

The third issue is that of administrative burdens on faculty shoulders. Collegial management requires that there be some, but there are too many in some universities and perhaps in most of them. Complaints that there are too many committees and too much busywork are common in universities, often accompanied by the refrain that it is difficult to devote the required time to "real work" – teaching and research. Too often administration in universities is excessively driven by suspicion of authority and procedural fetishism resulting in the triumph of doing over getting done, in process over substance. The result is excessive bureaucracy, endless second guessing and, too often, avoidance of responsibility.

The issue of multiple identities is not unique to universities, but it is common in them. Recall that the themes reported by Pennock et al. in their study of senates and university governance included tension between roles and responsibilities of senate within university governance, and tension between individual and constituency interests, and those of the university as a whole.[8] The same person may be a senate member, a faculty member, a department head, and a member of the faculty union. A faculty member may be on the board of governors in whose name negotiations are conducted with the union of which she is a member. Examples are numerous. The point is that multiple identities are complex and may be in conflict that is not easily reconciled. Sometimes it may even be unrecognized.

These issues raised by the juxtaposition of university governance and collegial management have several implications. Among them is the need for collegial management in the interest of the university as a whole, and recognition that the university can set standards that require adherence across all academic units. This does not mean that deans, provosts, and presidents acquire more top-down authority. Typically collegial management at the university level is exercised by committees, as it is at the departmental level. It does, however, mean that unit-level collegial management must conform to the standards prescribed by the university as a whole. It also means that deans and presidents must exercise the statutory authority given to them by law. The next section of this chapter will demonstrate that this authority is not always conceded within the academy.

Consider, now, the complexity added to governance and collegial management by collective bargaining regimes. The importation from the industrial world of a model of employer-employee relations that would have been seen at one time as anathema to the idea of a community of scholars is a development of fundamental importance. It encroaches on governance and collegial management and challenges their authority. Its full impact is not yet understood.

There is irony in the fact that institutions that prize their autonomy would adopt an external model that attenuates their freedom. Union status does not come without strings attached; there are many obligations rooted in labour legislation that now have become part of the body of law and policy embedded in university affairs. In addition, faculty unions may affiliate with larger labour organizations in ways that involve reciprocal obligations. For example, the University of Saskatchewan Faculty Association is an affiliate member of the Saskatchewan Federation of Labour and is obliged to subscribe to the federation's constitution, rules, and regulations. In turn, the federation is constitutionally empowered "to coordinate and promote the interests of its affiliates,"[9] a provision that may explain the most intrusive attempt to influence the university's affairs in recent history. In an effort to address irregularities in the labour studies program mounted by the College of Commerce (now the Edwards School of Business), the dean and I encountered the president of the Saskatchewan Federation of Labour (SFL) who claimed three prerogatives in this program. Control over admissions was one: the SFL president thought it important that the program serve labour activists only; managerial and administrative employees would, in his view, silence those with a labour background. A veto on the appointment of the program's executive director was another; and approval of the curriculum by the federation was the third. An NDP Cabinet minister contacted the university to reinforce the SFL president's claim to these prerogatives. Of course the claim was unacceptable for a program supported by the operating budget of a public university, and when the dean and I realized that the program's staff had bent or acquiesced to the federation's influence in these matters, the program was discontinued.[10]

Not all universities have imported this model into their internal affairs. A review of international rankings reveals that top-ranked institutions do not have faculty unions. Nor do the Canadian universities that feature most prominently in these rankings. The University of Toronto Faculty Association is the professional organization of the university's faculty and staff; the non-unionized McGill Association of University Teachers "functions within the collegial framework of academic life at McGill";[11] the University of British Columbia Faculty Association is a registered non-profit society incorporated under the province's Society Act; the McMaster University Faculty Association is a professional association; the University of Alberta has an Association of Academic Staff that derives its authority from the province's Post Secondary Learning Act. They have some of the same representative obligations in negotiating salaries and benefits, and representing members, as their unionized counterparts in other Canadian universities, but these obligations and their concomitant behaviours are not shaped by external labour laws and trade union cultures. They see themselves as professional associations, and the legal and cultural divide between them and faculty associations that are certified trade unions is wide.

There are many dimensions to the organization of faculty in unions, but two in particular merit early mention. First, in gaining union status, professors forfeit any claim to being a self-governing profession.[12] They confirm their status as employees, and an employer–employee relationship is different – in law and in fact – from other workplace relationships. Second, the most important and prominent feature of this relationship is the mutual obligation to engage in collective bargaining, an activity that not only is externally regulated but one that can be an uneasy fit with proclaimed ideals of universities. "Collective bargaining is not just another form of the search for truth in the university setting. It is about power, about one side having it and the other wanting some. And it is not decided by logic or research or even passion. It is decided by the mobilization and exercise of strength."[13]

Power struggles are very different from debates about competing claims to truth, but the latter is at the heart of the academic mission. Whether in the context of commercial opportunities or other temptations, universities rightly claim that the integrity of the academy must be protected. Universities require trust and respect, and if they are seen to bend in their mission before the influence of money or other extraneous factors, they risk losing both, because they have compromised the evidence-based search for truth for which they claim a unique status in our society. But what of institutional behaviours that favour power over truth? In labour strife, as in war, the first casualty is truth, and there is no exception for universities. Slogans, spin, and often the demonization of opponents[14] move to centre stage, and the performance is public. In the early days of any faculty strike in the country, and regardless of local issues, the Canadian Association of University Teachers and its faculty union members can be counted on to issue statements of solidarity with the striking union. Careful observers can see that adherence to the values of truth, reason, and evidence-based debate has yielded to a greater interest in winning a power struggle. This is seen as hypocrisy, and rightly so.

The problem for Canadian universities is that the power struggle is expanding in scope. The Canadian Association of University Teachers challenges historical governance arrangements on the basis that collective bargaining should be the process by which governance bodies are regulated. Its policy statement on the subject states, "The Board and Senate should operate within the context of procedures and rules set out in legislation constituting the institution and in collective agreements negotiated between the institution and its academic staff."[15]

Legislation does little more than provide for a board and senate and assign financial and academic oversight to them. According to this policy statement, the process for deciding how this oversight would be exercised should be collective bargaining. It is to draw a very long bow to suggest that the terms and conditions of employment, which are the normal business of collective bargaining, include how boards and senates should do the jobs assigned to them by the legislature. The policy statement is clearly a claim for faculty unions to have a role that extends beyond terms of employment to governance. And the role for which the claim is made is not a modest one. In the first instance it would subject the bylaws, rules, and regulations now made by boards and senates themselves to review through the collective bargaining process. It has the potential to go further and to advance a superintending role for faculty unions in governance generally. The origins of this claim lie in the CAUT view that senates have failed, not simply that they have weaknesses or are not living up to their potential, and the way forward is to recognize that collective bargaining is, and has proven to be, the best and most reliable way to secure the proper academic staff role in academic decision making.[16]

This means that for CAUT the role for collective bargaining in academic matters is potentially without limit. "Because academic staff are the effective agents for the execution of the research and educational functions of the academy our working environment and our terms and conditions of employment are inseparable from academic policies and objectives. Academic staff have a legal entitlement to engage in the collective bargaining of all their terms and conditions of employment."[17]

On this view, terms and conditions of employment include what legislatures have expressly entrusted to senates. The line in the sand is clear. A struggle of fundamental importance to the future of our universities is underway. We can turn to the case law to mark its progress. One important case[18] involved a decision by the president of the University of British Columbia not to recommend a faculty member for promotion from associate to full professor. The applicable BC provincial legislation provides that the university's board of governors has the power to appoint and to promote professors on the recommendation of the president.[19] A collective agreement between the university and faculty association contains terms and conditions governing the appointment, reappointment, tenure, and promotion of faculty and stipulates that decisions about them are subject to grievance and grievance arbitration under the agreement.

The faculty member's case for promotion proceeded through the various levels of decision-making provided for in the collective agreement: from departmental committee to dean, in consultation with an advisory committee, to president. Recommendations to the president are reviewed by a senior appointments committee, which makes its own recommendation before the final decision on whether a recommendation is to go to the board of governors is made by the president. When the president made her decision not to recommend promotion, the faculty association filed a grievance alleging that her decision was wrong as a result of procedural error and that it was unreasonable.

The arbitrator, a Vancouver lawyer, agreed with the faculty association on both counts. The question, now, was one of remedy, and on this subject the collective agreement provided that in procedural error resulting in a wrong decision, the arbitrator could direct reconsideration of the case, or decide it herself if it could not fairly be reconsidered; and that on a finding of unreasonableness, she must reverse the decision. But what then? The university argued that *reverse* meant "revoke or annul," together with a remission of the case back to the university for reconsideration. The arbitrator did not agree and interpreted *reverse* to mean that her decision to recommend promotion had to be substituted for the president's decision not to do so.

The university applied to the Labour Relations Board for leave to have the arbitrator's decision reconsidered and was unsuccessful. This prompted an application for judicial review to the Supreme Court of British Columbia, which also was unsuccessful. For sound policy reasons, decisions of arbitrators and of expert administrative tribunals such as labour relations boards are protected by privative clauses that allow them to be challenged only on a high standard. The standard in this case, ruled the British Columbia Supreme Court, was patent unreasonableness, which meant that both decisions would stand unless it could be shown they were made (a) arbitrarily or in bad faith, (b) for an improper purpose, (c) based entirely or predominantly on irrelevant factors, or (d) failing to take statutory requirements into account.[20] "The arbitrator's decision involved an interpretation of the collective agreement itself and a selection of the appropriate remedy pursuant to that agreement and the facts of the case. The discretion to choose the remedy is a matter clearly within the exclusive jurisdiction of the arbitrator protected by the privative clause and the standard of review of such a decision would be patent unreasonableness. The Board's decision ... was to consider whether the decision was consistent with the principles of the Code. Their decision that it was, is not patently unreasonable."[21]

There things stood before an appeal to British Columbia's highest court. The preamble to the decision of that court is set out here in full so that the real issue for universities is understood. The question is not whether a tenure decision is sound or otherwise, and it is not whether the faculty association or university administration is correct in its views of a case. Nor is the question whether the arbitrator or Labour Relations Board was correct in any matter of law or fact before it. The issue for universities is the decision they have made to subject their academic processes to a potential for this degree of external intervention. The university president's recommendation following extensive internal consideration of a tenure case could be overturned by an external arbitrator who concluded that it was unreasonable. But that arbitrator's decision to substitute her view on tenure for that of the university president was final unless found to be patently unreasonable. Entertaining the potential for intrusiveness on this scale is odd behaviour by institutions that prize their autonomy.

The last judicial words on this case came with a decision of the British Columbia Court of Appeal in April 2007 allowing a UBC appeal against the judicial review decision, and with a refusal of the Supreme Court of Canada to allow a further appeal to that court by the UBC Faculty Association.[22] The majority of the Court of Appeal held that an incorrect standard of review was applied by the Labour Relations Board and the lower court decision. Because the case required a legal interpretation of the University Act, it fell outside the area in which the Labour Relations Board could claim exclusive jurisdiction by virtue of the privative clause, and was reviewable by the courts. The interpretation of the University Act and "the determination and resolution of any operational conflict between the collective agreement and the University Act had to be correct."[23]

The faculty association's central argument throughout was that the president's statutory authority to recommend appointments, promotions, and dismissals could be limited by a collective agreement, and that is what happened when the parties agreed that an arbitrator could reverse the president's decision if she found it to be unreasonable. But, said the Court of Appeal, "by s. 28(2) of the University Act, the President's recommendation is a necessary condition to the Board of Governor's exercise of its statutory authority to make appointments ... Similarly, by s. 28(3) the president's recommendation is a necessary condition to the Board of Governor's exercise of its statutory authority to promote or remove a member of the teaching staff. The language used in both subsections ... is mandatory."[24] It was therefore not open to the arbitrator to substitute her recommendation for that of the president, and the Court of Appeal remitted the matter of the promotion to the president for reconsideration, the only remedy consistent with the University Act.

Another recent and related case continues in Saskatchewan. A tenure case was heard at the different levels of decision-making provided for in the collective agreement between the University of Saskatchewan and its faculty association: departmental, college, and university review committees, and a tenure appeal committee. The results were in support of tenure at the departmental and appeal committees and against it in the college and university review committees. The president[25] determined that the professor did not meet the tenure standards for research and scholarly work, and advised her that he would not recommend tenure but that he would extend her probationary period for two years.

The faculty association grieved the decision,[26] claiming that the president should not have rejected the application and also that he should not have met with the university's academic vice-provost before making his decision. The arbitrator who heard the grievance determined that the president's recommendation was required by statute in order for tenure to be granted, and that his meeting with the vice-provost did not result in a breach of procedural fairness, because the president did not hear new information at that meeting, nor did he discuss the substance of the tenure case with the vice-provost.

The faculty association applied for judicial review to the Saskatchewan Court of Queen's Bench, where the judge held for procedural reasons that the arbitrator did not have jurisdiction. Subsequently, the president's recommendation went to the university's board of governors and tenure was denied. Following the expiry of the extended probation period, during which no new tenure application was received, the professor was advised that her appointment was concluded. The faculty association proceeded with a second grievance following this decision. The association argued that there is no collective agreement requirement that the president recommend a candidate for tenure and that his role was limited to transmitting the recommendation of the appeal committee to the board. At issue were provisions of the University of Saskatchewan Act and Collective Agreement as follows:

University Act

73(1) The president is responsible for supervising and directing: (a) the academic work of the university, its faculty members and student body and its officers and employees employed in connection with that work; and (b) the business affairs of the university and its officers and employees employed in connection with those affairs ...

73(3) The president shall: ... (b) make recommendations to the board respecting the appointment, promotion or removal of any faculty member or any of its officers or employees ...

Powers of the Board:

49(1) The Board may: ... (j) subject to section ... 51, appoint the president, the vice-presidents, the secretary, the faculty members and any other officers and employees that are required to be appointed by this act ...

51 For the purpose of clause 49(1) (j): (a) no person is to be appointed as a faculty member unless that person has been nominated for the position by the president; and (b) no faculty member is to be promoted or removed from office except on the recommendation of the president ...

Collective Agreement

15(3) ... Tenure is granted only by the Board acting in accordance with the provisions of his agreement. The decision of the Board is final and there shall be no appeal within the University against the Board's decision other than resort to the grievance procedure ...

15(13) Renewals and Tenure Appeal Committee: Powers and procedures: ... By March 31, meetings and deliberations shall be concluded, decisions rendered and recommendations made to the President for transmission to the Board.

The faculty association's argument was simply this: the president's role is limited by collective agreement section 15(13) to transmission of the decision of the tenure appeal committee to the board of governors. He or she does not make a recommendation in the matter. The university's reply is that sections 73(1) and 73(3) confer on the president a broad mandate in academic as well as business affairs, and a specific mandate to make recommendations in personnel matters, specifically appointments, promotions, and dismissals. A secondary faculty association argument was that tenure is not specifically mentioned in the legislation; even if the president has authority to make recommendations in other matters enumerated in the legislation, he may not do so in the case of tenure, the single most important personnel decision made by any university.

There is a subtext underlying the faculty association's argument that should not be missed. The president transmits the tenure appeal committee's decision to the board. What does the board do with it? The president is precluded by the collective agreement from making a recommendation; indeed it is not clear he can even express an opinion that may be at variance with the decision. Even if he could, that opinion cannot prevail with the board. Despite the clear authority of the board to award tenure, it is effectively precluded from making its own decision. It cannot conduct its own hearing; it cannot hear a recommendation to the contrary from its president. The board would have to act always on the only decision before it – that of the tenure appeal committee – even if its own view and the views of its senior academic advisors are to the contrary. In this subtext the board's authority is hollow, and that is the intention.

If the faculty association argument prevails, it would mean that the intent and language of the University of Saskatchewan Act could be negated by the employment contract. Of course the act could be amended and the word *tenure* could be added to sections 73(3) and

51(b), but that would address only the association's secondary argument. The primary argument remains: the board must abide by the decision of the tenure appeal committee. It cannot as a practical matter conduct its own hearing, nor can it hear a recommendation from its most senior officer, the university president, and his chief academic advisor, the provost: collective agreement trumps legislation.

Of course it can be said that the administration was unwise to entertain this state of affairs when the collective agreement was negotiated, and that is true. But it is an incomplete answer to the effective negation of legislative intent by an employment contract. The legislation assigned a substantive role to the administration and board in these decisions, one that is in keeping with recognized practice. "Tenure is not an item lightly to be conferred, for the granting of tenure is likely to shape the university's future for years to come."[27]

Matters of such importance rightly engage the attention of the university's senior academic officers – president and provost – and they rightly command the attention of the board to their recommendations and advice. "Recommendations by the committee, department head, and dean are usually not binding. The institution's chief academic officer (provost, vice-chancellor, vice-president for academic affairs) normally has (for all practical purposes) the final authority to … grant tenure."[28]

To remove the capacity of president and provost to recommend to the recognized decision-making body – the board of governors – is effectively to deny both board and senior administration a role in the most important personnel decisions of the university.

As important as the British Columbia and Saskatchewan cases are to the universities directly concerned, they have a wider significance for all Canadian universities. These cases are not exceptional or peculiar and they are not, as lawyers like to say, limited to their own facts. The faculty association positions in both cases are consistent with the CAUT view, described above, that encourages a further encroachment of collective bargaining upon governance. University boards, senates, and administrations should resist this encroachment and reverse it where it already has taken place.

Faculty unions will argue (1) that university administrations have adopted a top-down, corporate model of administration, thereby requiring faculty associations to seek greater power through collective bargaining; (2) (and related to 1), that senates have become weakened in influence, prompting faculty unions to act in their stead as the voice of the academy; and (3) that unions negotiate process only, leaving the substance of academic decisions in academic hands. On the first argument, university administrations have not acquired more power in a formal sense, though they do not behave as they did decades ago. In most cases their universities have become large and complex organizations, and with size and complexity come bureaucracy and a more managerial culture. Administration may be more remote than once it was, but collegial management remains at the core of university organization. The formation of faculty unions is not about the reacquisition of power once lost; faculty have not become workers, with their colleagues in administration the bosses. Faculty remain collegial decision-makers with great discretion over how they organize their lives and do their work. Their unions do not need to displace senates to give them greater voice and power.

The second and related argument – that weak senates point to the need for collective bargaining to lead in academic matters – is also flawed. It is a generalization without compelling evidence. The survey conducted by Pennock et al.[29] reports issues that need to be addressed for senates to be more effective, but it does not support the apocalyptic judgment that they have failed. The senate at my university (University Council) is a far more effective body than it was decades ago. Other universities would report diverse experience, no doubt some better, others worse. The blanket judgment, however, is not supported.

The third argument resting on discrete spheres of process and substance should have been seen as discredited years ago. Process frames and often determines substance. The procedures that are negotiated in a collective agreement will influence and often drive outcomes, as illustrated by the British Columbia and Saskatchewan cases considered above. It was inevitable that under the UBC collective agreement an external decision-maker would sooner or later overrule the university president in the matter of tenure. And in the Saskatchewan case, the negotiated obligation of the president to transmit a recommendation of an internal tribunal to the board of governors without advising the board of his own recommendation and opinion meant that in practice the board – the acknowledged and lawful decision-making body – had no choice but to accept the recommendation of the internal tribunal. The idea that collective agreements address process only and leave substance in the hands of others is naive.

If the reasons claimed in support of CAUT-inspired initiatives for collective bargaining to supersede senate governance do not withstand scrutiny, the related question must be asked: are there good reasons why these initiatives should be resisted, as distinct from looked upon with indifference? We already have considered one, of course, and it is that legislatures have conferred upon senates authority in academic matters. Public authorities should not be expected to ignore efforts to tilt the scales away from senates in favour of collective bargaining. University autonomy does not go so far as to mean that universities are free to make whatever internal arrangements they like – through collective bargaining or otherwise – about their governance. That is a matter for public statute, and governments will not and should not stand idly by while their legislation is being hollowed out. If public universities want to court intrusion by government into their affairs, unwise collective bargaining that negates or diminishes the statute that provides for their governance is a good way to do it.

This is not the only reason. From the standpoint both of organization and process, faculty unions and collective bargaining are ill suited for significant roles in university governance. The former have obligations to represent their members, both in securing more favourable terms and conditions of employment, and in providing them with representation if and when they face the prospect of sanction for alleged shortcomings or misbehaviours in connection with their employment. It matters that their duties include terms and conditions of employment and representing their members in difficult times, but do not include university governance. Senates and boards have responsibility for the latter, and it is a principle of sound governance that authority should accompany responsibility. It is an equally sound principle that in the absence of responsibility, one should have neither the authority nor the opportunity. Simply put, university governance is not the faculty union's responsibility.

This is not to deny the prerogative to criticize the board, senate, and administration. And of course leaders and members of the union may also be members of the board or senate, in which case they may have governance responsibility, but they have it as members of those bodies, not as members of the union. They may and do have trouble "changing their hats" sometimes, but that is not uncommon when people have two or more duties that are different and may even put them in conflict.

And conflict is common, though too often its acknowledgment is not. A faculty member has an interest in her union's negotiation of a higher salary increase, and she may be a member of the board forced

in times of financial stringency to resist it. The conflict may not be satisfactorily avoided by leaving the boardroom at voting time. A faculty
union leader committed to the CAUT governance agenda may also be
a member of the senate, the very body that he is committed to diminish
in order to secure a prominent governance role for his union. This is an
egregious conflict of interest.

Underlying these considerations is another, that of culture. It is fair
to say that university administrations have become more managerial
in culture. It is also fair to say that faculty unions have evolved to take
on more of the culture of the labour movement. It is a culture that is
an uneasy fit within universities. Fundamentally, unions are driven by
egalitarian considerations and have an impulse to see everyone treated
equally, which in their lexicon means the same. Universities are meri-
tocracies, or at least they like to claim they are, with the difficult responsibility of making judgments about relative merits, of their students certainly, but if they are living up to their claim, of their colleagues as well,
and their relative contributions to advancing the university's effectiveness and reputation.

If their organization as unions militates against faculty associations
taking on more governance responsibility, so too does the most important process by which they do their work. Collective bargaining is about
working out an employment contract. It is not about identifying the best
interests of the university; nor is it the relative truth about the claims of
either union or management. It is about the give and take, the push and
pull, and the concessions sought and made to reach an agreement. This
is not a forum in which to introduce the additional task of negotiating
governance. The opposite is the case: it is a forum to be avoided in the
interest of good governance.

Governments should make it clear to public universities with faculty unions that they will not tolerate encroachment through collective bargaining upon governance arrangements set out in legislation or charters. These universities should be reminded that their
self-governance is in the public interest, and that governments will
intervene to protect that interest if legislative authority is undermined or compromised by collective bargaining. Indeed the time
may have come for governments to consider a legislative framework
that delineates the boundaries between the two. This framework
would emphasize that "terms and conditions of employment" open
to collective bargaining must be construed so as to leave unhindered
the legislature's prerogative to provide for the statutory authority

of boards, senates, and their responsible officers. Such a framework should pay particular attention to the definition of academic matters that ought to be within the purview of academic senates. In addition to approval and oversight of academic programs, oversight of the standards, rules, and procedures for awarding tenure and promotion should remain squarely in the purview of the governing bodies.

Chapter Seven

A Canadian Dilemma: Strong Science, Weak Innovation

University presidents are storytellers. They tell the stories of their universities in hundreds of settings, formal and informal, near and far. These are accounts of achievements, usually of faculty, whose work has had a powerful and enduring impact on the institution, and they are told to remind listeners about its finest hours and to inspire them to emulate the example. One of my favourite stories is that of Nobel Prize laureate Gerhard Herzberg who in 1935 found refuge at the University of Saskatchewan from the Nazi regime in his native Germany. His decade on faculty was a key link in the causal chain that led to the university's successful bid to attract the Canadian Light Source (CLS) more than a half-century later.

Herzberg was both physicist and chemist and in his time the most outstanding molecular spectroscopist in the world. He used this scientific technique to analyse matter, to measure wavelengths of light absorbed or emitted by molecules, and thereby to identify their structure. He was a leading figure in developing the university's strength in structural science. A betatron was secured by the physics department in 1948 and used in nuclear research and cancer treatment, leading in 1951 to the installation of a cobalt-60 unit – first of many in the world that have been used to treat millions of cancer patients. This capacity led in 1964 to the opening of a linear accelerator laboratory, which in turn led to the successful synchrotron bid inspired and led by accelerator laboratory director Dennis Skopik. The accelerator is now incorporated as a component part – the electron gun – of the Canadian Light Source.

The Light Source is Canada's national synchrotron research establishment. This synchrotron is a laboratory the size of a football field in which electromagnetic radiation (or light) is generated into a diverse array of beamlines and used to study the structural and chemical properties of materials at the molecular level. It has been compared to a giant microscope, and its scientific uses are numerous. Canadian scientists had pursued the idea of a synchrotron in the country since 1972, but it was not until the spring of 1999 that construction of "the largest scientific facility in Canada"[1] in thirty years was announced, representing "an unprecedented level of collaboration among governments, universities and industry in Canada."[2]

Although I was not involved in bringing the synchrotron to the U of S,[3] I became president before the first sod was turned in the construction of the $173-million facility,[4] and for several years I was close to its construction and early development phases. This experience brought me into the world of Canadian science policy and to an understanding of the prominent role it will have in determining the future success of our country. Are we on the path to success or one to a less favourable destination?

There has been no shortage of national self-assessment on science, technology, and related matters in Canada; we have seen several studies in the past decade alone.[5] Three of the most comprehensive are the 2008 and 2010 state of the nation reports produced by the Science, Technology and Innovation Council of Canada[6] and the 2012 report on science and technology prepared by an expert panel assembled by the Council of Canadian Academies.[7] What is at stake is outlined in the introduction to the 2008 Report: "Strength and leadership in Science Technology and innovation ... is the price of entry to full participation in the knowledge-based global economy of the 21st century. To thrive in the new global economy, a country must innovate. Deep and comprehensive capacities to discover, create, source, adopt and market new goods and services underpin our country's future economic growth and each citizen's quality of life. Improvements in our health, personal security, and the quality of our environment all go hand in hand with our ability to innovate."[8]

"Discover, create, source, adopt and market": these verbs convey the reality that innovation is a process and not an event. Processes have steps or stages, and the 2008 report recorded Canadian success or progress in some of these stages, and our shortcomings in others. The report identifies and publishes benchmark comparisons in three areas: business innovation, knowledge development and transfer, and talent development. The first reveals a paradox that has been known and unresolved for some time: Canadian government support of business research and development is among the highest in the comparison group of OECD and G7 countries, but it has not produced results commensurate with the investment. In general, the report tells us, "in relative terms, we are falling behind our major competitors, and the gap is growing ... most Canadian industrial sectors are less capital intensive than those in the U.S."[9] We spend less than our competitors on machinery and equipment, and the equipment we do use more often than not is developed elsewhere: "More than 55 percent of manufacturing plants that introduce advanced technologies to the market in Canada are most likely to be technology purchasers."[10] Venture capital investments – as a percentage of gross domestic product – lag behind major competitors, and Canadian investments in VC tend to be in retail venture capital companies, as distinct from direct investments in start-ups.[11]

Why is there a discrepancy between public investment and results? Neither this report nor others are definitive on reasons, but one clue is to be found in the difference between indirect and direct investment in research and development: "90 percent of Canadian support was for indirect measures (the business R&D tax credit) while 80 percent of government support in the U.S. was for direct government funding of Business Enterprise Research and Development (BERD), and only 20 percent of U.S. government support of business R&D went for indirect measures."[12] The difference is important: "Many leading countries in innovation rely much less than Canada on indirect tax incentives as opposed to direct measures."[13] But the subject is complex, and other variables, including cultural differences, cannot be overlooked.[14]

Knowledge development and transfer is the subject of the second set of indicators in the 2008 report. Here, Canada fares better, at least in knowledge development. "Canadian universities are a key component of the national innovation system ... Whether measured as a share of total national R&D or as a share of GDP, the university sector's contribution to national R&D in Canada is larger than that of most OECD and G-7 countries."[15]

Knowledge transfer is another matter, and in this area the results are mixed. While "Canadian businesses fund university research to a higher degree than in other countries,"[16] collaboration between businesses and universities on R&D is low by international standards, and licensing revenues in Canadian universities are lower than in their American counterparts. While in the past Canadian universities produced a higher rate of research-based spin-off companies, numbers have dropped in recent years.[17]

Benchmark comparisons for talent development are also mixed. Our youth have high aptitude for science, math, and reading, but 40 per cent of working-age Canadians lack the skills required for a knowledge-based economy, and "our track record of investing in training in the workplace has also been poor over the past decade."[18] University enrolment in business-related fields is low, related to other countries.

That was in 2008. The 2010 "State of the Nation Report"[19] focused on weaknesses identified in its predecessor. In asking "How good is Canada's science, technology and innovation system at delivering the outcomes we want?,"[20] it records that our talent pool is "holding its own" with growth in numbers of university graduates, and master's and doctoral graduates in science and engineering. Our youth continue to perform well in science, math and reading.[21] But "transferring knowledge from research institutions in universities and government to the marketplace and building a culture of innovation in business remain paths requiring attention."[22] R&D performed by business remained low by international standards and declined between the 2008 and 2010 reports.[23] The challenge remains "to deploy talent well, invest in advanced technology, integrate innovation into corporate and country strategies and leverage our efforts to deliver prosperity for all Canadians."[24]

The Expert Panel in 2012 concluded that Canadian science and technology "is healthy and growing"[25] and in support of this assessment reported (1) that with 0.5 per cent of the world's population, "Canada produces 4.1 percent of the world's scientific papers and nearly 5 percent of the world's most frequently cited papers. In 2005–10 Canada produced 59 percent more papers than in 1999–2004, and was the only G7 country with an increase above the world average."[26]

There is quality as well as quantity. Bibliometric measures of the frequency of paper citation placed Canada sixth in the world – among the top five in seven of twenty-two research fields measured, and the top ten in a further fourteen fields.[27] Bibliometrics are supported by a survey of the authors of most frequently cited papers who placed Canada fourth overall in the world.[28]

Again it is reported that knowledge creation is not matched by knowledge transfer and an increase in innovation. Sometimes this issue is explored in terms of pure and applied research, but this language is not helpful: "Most research is either performed with a commercial or social application as an objective in the short or longer term, or finds such application even when not envisioned at the time the research was performed."[29] Patent activity is an important indicator in comparing national science and technology outputs. Invention disclosures, royalty and licensing revenues, spin-off activities and companies, new products and services, and university-business partnerships are others.[30]

Given Canada's low business expenditure on research and development, we should expect to find correspondingly low patent activity. Although Canada produces more than 4 per cent of the world's total scientific publications, in 2009 it accounted for only 1.28 per cent of sets of patents filed with the European Patent Office, the US Patent and Trademark Office, and the Japan Patent Office.[31] "Moreover, Canada's overall share of world patents has fallen since 2005. The United States' share of total patents has also declined, but many other developed countries – including Germany, France, Sweden, Japan, and the United Kingdom – increased their share of world patents over the same period. China had the largest increase ... Canada also ranks poorly in patents on a per capita basis, with a level that is well below the OECD average."[32]

Canada lags, too, in royalties and licensing fees related to intellectual property and is a net exporter of IP.[33] Further, as previously noted, our country fares poorly in venture capital investments – particularly for start-ups – and the number of spin-off companies has dropped in recent years.

The reports of the Science, Technology, and Innovation Council and the Council of Canadian Academies are supplemented by other important studies dealing with Canadian innovation. In 2007 the Conference Board of Canada placed Canada fourteenth out of seventeen peer countries in innovation, which it defines as "a process through which economic or social value is extracted from knowledge – through the creating, diffusing and transforming of ideas – to produce new or improved products, services, processes, strategies or capabilities."[34] "Canada is well supplied with good universities, engineering schools, teaching hospitals, and technical institutes. It produces science that is well respected around the world. But, with some exceptions, Canada does not take the steps that other countries take to ensure research can be successfully commercialized and used as a source of advantage for innovative companies seeking global market share. Canadian companies are thus rarely at the leading edge of new technology and too often find themselves a generation or more behind the productivity growth achieved by global industry leaders."[35]

And on the subject of productivity, in its 2008 report the Competition Review Panel cited the "deeply troubling fact that Canada's productivity growth had lagged behind that of most industrialized countries over a 25-year period." The panel "linked much of Canada's poor productivity performance to the comparatively poor performance of Canadian companies in the creation, diffusion and transformation of knowledge and the use of knowledge through commercialization."[36]

These five reports on Canadian innovation are hardly revelations. By the 1980s, "Canada had never had a national science policy."[37] Universities produced "basic research," which, it was assumed, would in due course lead to economic returns that might be neither anticipated nor planned. This was the "linear model of innovation,"[38] and its "dominant metaphor"[39] is the pipeline or pipe. "Fundamental discoveries are fed into one end of the pipe and move through various stages of development until they emerge onto the market at the far end of the pipe. The resultant growth fuels the economy and returns taxes ... It was argued that government investment in basic research must be preserved and that science must be left to regulate itself if the pipeline was to fuel the innovation process and produce wealth."[40]

In Canada and elsewhere this metaphor was "the foundation of the postwar 'social contract for science,' a contract secured by a promissory note on the eventual but completely unpredictable technological and social spin-offs of basic science."[41] However, if serendipity is to be the basis for science policy it must be shown to work, and the reports summarized above demonstrate that in Canada it has not worked, at least not well. Either the metaphor of pipelines was inapt or we had failed to build them.

The creation of the Networks of Centres of Excellence (NCEs) in 1989 marked a decisive shift in the direction of a more strategic approach and was "the most dramatic change in Canadian science policy since the National Research Council was established in 1916 ... The federal government envisaged a web of national research networks – 'research institutes without walls' anchored in academic settings – that in partnership with the private sector would target and develop practical and commercial applications. These twin facts – practical goals and distributed networks – were unprecedented and highly controversial at the time. Now, they are central themes of contemporary science policy ... Scientific excellence, commercial relevance, and public-private collaborations are recurrent themes in all new programs."[42]

As Janet Atkinson-Grosjean observed in 2006, the novelty of this decisive shift in policy should command our attention, and she asks,

"How are macro-level changes in policy ... playing out at the micro-level of the university or hospital laboratory?" To answer the question, she undertook a case study of the Canadian Genetic Diseases Network (CGDN), which at the time of her study consisted of fifty scientists, eleven universities and hospitals, and eight companies.[43] Its program covered four themes: gene identification, pathogenesis and functional genomics, genetic therapies, and genetics and health care.[44] The network was incorporated in 1998 to accelerate commercial progress before its funding cap in 2005. At this time 70 per cent of its funding went to fundamental, discovery-based research; 20 per cent to early stage technologies with commercial potential; and 10 per cent to networking and administration.[45] Atkinson-Grosjean describes how the progress of her study revealed issues at the intersection of public and private science: "The tension between the public and private faces of NCEs became increasingly apparent over the course of the study. Alternating currents of confidentiality and openness ebbed and flowed around the project. Scientists spoke to me freely, while gatekeepers erected barricades. The contradictions and barriers to access illustrated the normative and ethical boundaries that are constantly negotiated in this world."[46]

Commercial sensitivity was at the roots of this tension. Private participants and funders of the network seek to protect their investment by preventing disclosure to competitors, an understandable interest but one in conflict with the value accorded to openness in scholarly investigation. But as Atkinson-Grosjean observes, these are differences to be negotiated, not barriers to prevent the initiative from moving forward.

Atkinson-Grosjean's case study leads her to six conclusions: (1) Instead of the common and dichotomous basic/applied research distinction, and the linear process implied by the pipeline metaphor, it is more helpful to speak of translational research that is "dedicated to both understanding and use."[47] Defence research, agricultural research into new crop varieties, and biomedical research to identify new therapies are examples.[48] (2) There is translation to practice and translation to profit,[49] and the latter leads to tension, particularly if and when a research network is incorporated. Unincorporated networks depend upon universities, but once incorporated, they become distinct organizations with distinct missions. (3) Traditional academic values of collegiality, openness, and sharing of ideas prevail within the networks but not in their external relations, where knowledge is proprietary and treated as intellectual property. (4) It is difficult to assess the impact of the more than $2 billion committed to the NCE program (at the time of her writing in 2006) because the value added is incalculable, though program advantages of higher quality research, improved collaboration, and resources located at core facilities are themselves added value. (5) There is a blurring of public/private when "public" networks are funded to generate "private" goods, though NCEs and universities "internalize the private sector by protecting their own IP and creating companies to exploit it."[50] (6) And finally, "There is danger in focusing on scientific excellence and commercial relevance to the exclusion other criteria. Relevance is social as well as economic. The economic interpretation, however, has been the predominant concern of the NCE program."[51]

These conclusions have important public policy implications. "Since networks are becoming the default institutional structures in which public science is performed, and since public scientists are undertaking more and more adventures in the nature of trade, accountability is a valid concern. Policy makers perhaps need to reassess and reassert their expectations of what is properly open and properly closed, whether in public or private science."[52]

In "Innovation Canada: A Call to Action," an expert panel reviewed federal support for research and development. The panel's report was eagerly awaited, because its mandate was to build on the reports of the Council of Canadian Academies and the Science, Technology, and Innovation Council and to suggest ways of improving Canada's performance – that is, to recommend solutions. The panel began by acknowledging the problem: "Studies have repeatedly documented that business innovation in Canada lags behind other highly developed countries. This gap is of vital concern because innovation is the ultimate source of the long-term competitiveness of businesses and the quality of life of Canadians."[53]

The panel's framework for action encompassed six recommendations: (1) creation of an Industrial Research and Innovation Council as the key body focused on innovation, including strategy, program delivery, and oversight or assessment of other federal, business-related programs; (2) changes to the Scientific Research and Experimental Development (SR&ED) program to narrow its base and generate savings to be redirected for direct investments in small and medium-size enterprises; (3) establishment of risk capital funds to facilitate access by innovation-based Canadian businesses to risk capital at start-up and later stages; (4) dismantling of the National Research Council by making its business-oriented institutes "independent collaborative research organizations, intended to be focal points for sectoral research and innovation strategies with the private sector"[54] (NRC institutes that perform fundamental research would affiliate with universities, and those with public policy emphasis would be transferred to related federal departments and agencies); (5) making innovation a stated objective of procurement policy and programs; and (6) establishing business innovation as a "whole-of-government priority," with ministerial responsibility for putting innovation "at the centre of the government's economic strategy and to engage the provinces in a dialogue on innovation to improve coordination and impact."[55]

In 2013 the Council of Canadian Academies released a report on industrial R&D in Canada.[56] Other reports had noted our weak performance in this "critical driver of innovation"[57] and had speculated upon reasons for it, but a more systematic study with this focus was needed. The findings pointed to IR&D strengths in aerospace, information and communications technology, oil and gas extraction, and pharmaceutical and medicine manufacturing. In general, however, the report found "limited alignment"[58] between our science and technology strengths, industrial research and development, and the Canadian economy. It identified "five barriers to translation of S&T knowledge into innovation and wealth creation":[59] ineffective technology transfer processes; shortage of managerial, commercialization, and organizational skills; little public funding for development and commercialization of new technologies ("Unlike other countries, the majority of public support for IR&D in Canada is provided through tax credits, rather than direct investments");[60] the absence of Canadian public procurement policies that favour IR&D; and business culture ("Canadian business leaders are risk averse relative to their U.S. counterparts").[61]

Reports, scholarly analyses, and recommendations are abundant. What is the prospect that they will lead to better public policy, which will result in improvement in Canadian innovation? To begin, we need a clear articulation of policy objectives and responsibility for achieving them, and this is a challenge for any state, let alone a federation as decentralized as ours. We are reluctant to declare high ambition, whether because we are unable to speak with one voice or we fear repercussions from falling short. Perhaps there is more to the amorphous cultural arguments than we care to admit: Canada is a solid, middle-of-the-pack performer because that is where Canadians are most comfortable. Even if true, however, middle-of-the-pack performance is no longer assured, if ever it was. The competitive forces amply documented in the reports summarized above warn us that our innovation shortcomings do not mean we stay the same; they mean that we risk decline in innovation, productivity, and standard of living.

For this reason, the sixth recommendation of the Jenkins panel may be its most important, because it speaks to improving coordination and impact though, we might add, not only between Ottawa and provinces, but between the public sector and the private, universities and industry, indeed among all participants in innovation. If we could imagine coordination on this scale, it is inconceivable that it would lead to contentment with the status quo. Surely we Canadians would say that our capacity, resources, and sheer good fortune should lead us to aspire to be among global leaders in innovation and to fashion policies to that end.

If the big question is answered and we know our ambition and goals, how do we realize them? We must begin by acknowledging the shortcomings documented in the reports already outlined and develop policies to address them. An illustrative example drawn from personal experience is the Canadian Light Source referenced at the beginning of this chapter: the operational funding of major science infrastructure.

No sooner had the first sod been turned on the construction of the synchrotron than the question became pressing: how are we going to operate this huge facility? The question had been asked earlier, though it had not been satisfactorily addressed by the University of Saskatchewan, other participating universities, governments, or other agencies. This was a major platform technology, and there were no policies in place or agencies responsible for addressing operational needs. And these were substantial – estimated to be approximately 10 per cent of capital costs per year – which, in the case of synchrotrons, increase as new suites of beamlines are added to the facility. The cost to date of the original structure and added beamlines is in excess of $350 million.

The extensive construction phase for this complicated and unique (in Canada) laboratory meant that we had some time to resolve the matter of operating costs before opening the door to the Canadian and international scientific communities. But we could not wait until then to begin our efforts, and so I began early to discuss the issue with federal officials in Ottawa. I did not meet with an enthusiastic response. "Why are you speaking to me?," said one senior official. "It's your synchrotron; it's your problem." There was resistance, too, to a description of the synchrotron as a national science facility, because the language itself suggested a federal government obligation to pay at least some of the operating costs. I was informed by senior public servants and by ministers that the federal government did not want to become involved in paying for the operations of major science installations.

The official was correct that the synchrotron was owned by the University of Saskatchewan, but university ownership was a requirement for capital funding from the Canada Foundation for Innovation, not a requirement or even a preference of the university. (I once offered to sell the facility to the federal government for one dollar on the condition that it commit to paying its operating costs.) Moreover, the federal government already was involved in paying the operating costs of at least one facility – Triumf in Vancouver – though this was not widely known because payment of its operating funds flowed through the National Research Council. The point was simple: what was the coherent reason for paying the operating costs of Canada's national laboratory for particle and nuclear physics and not doing so for Canada's national platform technology for synchrotron science?

I was not the only one asking this and related questions. The University of Victoria was the lead on Ocean Networks Canada, a cabled undersea network consisting of the Neptune and Venus arrays, designed and built to address questions about the earth's oceans. Its major research themes are earthquake and plate tectonics, fluid flow in the seabed, marine processes and climate change, deep-sea ecosystems, and engineering and data management. This was another big science project developed with the support of the Canada Foundation for Innovation and one that would extend the boundaries of traditional oceanography in addressing fundamental questions of ocean and earth science. University of Victoria president David Turpin had to ensure Neptune does what it is designed to do and not become an unused or underutilized artefact symbolizing science policy failure.

With the development of the Canada Foundation for Innovation it was inevitable that the Canadian Light Source and Neptune would be joined by more big science infrastructure. SNOLAB, an underground physics laboratory in Sudbury, and the Laval University–led icebreaker dedicated to Arctic Ocean research are others. The operating costs of these facilities are well beyond the capacities of their host institutions. They are platform technologies or they represent consortiums that extend well beyond their hosts to include broad membership from Canadian and international science communities. The question they present is fundamental: why invest hundreds of millions of public dollars in these big science technologies without ensuring that the resources are available to support their operations at levels required by scientific standards? If Canada cannot do this, leave it to others, and to those others will go the related scientific and innovation benefits.

It took years – and endless meetings in Ottawa – to begin to change the attitude first encountered in the nation's capital. In itself this was a problem. It is the job of university presidents to lead in advocacy for financial support for their institutions and entities such as CLS, but when the latter's CEOs – science leaders of the calibre of Bill Thomlinson and Josef Hormes[62] – have to join them in knocking on hundreds of Ottawa doors trying to change the minds of politicians and senior public servants, it detracts from the reason they were hired: to provide scientific leadership in the development of their facilities. This is wasteful.

Uncertainty too is a problem. The technical personnel at synchrotrons are highly specialized, and there is a global market for their talents. Recruiting and retaining these skilled and scarce people is a challenge that is compounded when there is uncertainty about financial stability. Not only must the money to operate a synchrotron be assured; it must be committed in a timely fashion to avoid the loss of specialists who are tempted by what they see as better prospects elsewhere in the world.

Slowly progress was made, in that sympathy replaced indifference as the problem of operating costs was explained and repeated. But we also confronted the fact that no department, agency, official, or politician would concede to a role in resolving the problem. "Yes, yes," would be the typical response, "we understand the issue, but it is not our mandate or responsibility to address it." It was no one's responsibility, because there was no policy or program in place or emergent, and no central agency charged with coordinating efforts to identify a solution. As the old saying goes, this was no way to run a railroad. And it was no way to develop major national science facilities.

As construction of the CLS advanced, the spectre of an official opening followed by an unofficial closing for want of operations funding began to have an impact. Finally, in March 2004 funding sufficient to operate the facility for its first five years could be identified through seven sources: NSERC, NRC, CIHR, Governments of Canada and Saskatchewan, University of Saskatchewan, and industrial users. After 2008–9, the Canada Foundation for Innovation became the eighth contributor through its infrastructure operating fund.

It should be clear what the issue here is. It is not to pay or to coordinate payment of operating costs without qualification or limits. It is to do so subject to peer review of performance and at levels commensurate with standards applicable to synchrotron research worldwide. This applies as well, in their different contexts, to Neptune, SNOLAB, Laval's ice-breaker, and other major science infrastructure. In the case of the Canadian Light Source, a multidisciplinary expert review committee ranked it "among the best in the world."[63] Operating funds sufficient to maintain this standard should not have to be assembled, agency by agency, starting from scratch each time in the shadows of uncertainty. Subject to peer review every five years, they should be available on a coordinated, predictable and timely basis.

The synchrotron case study illustrates the importance of the call from the Jenkins panel to improve coordination and impact, and the persistence of the issues that underlie it. Canadians do good science, but we need to improve science policy, the pathways to knowledge translation, and innovation policy. How do we do this?

First we need to acknowledge that what has been described variously as basic, fundamental, or curiosity-driven research is the sine qua non of translation and innovation. We need to keep doing good science, and to do so, we must fill in some gaps in science policy, including the one discussed above, identifying responsibility to coordinate funding for the operation of major science infrastructure. Another gap lies in the need for a satisfactory conclusion to the never-ending story of the indirect costs of research. To raise the matter in government circles invites the same reaction as to an off-colour joke in polite company. "Oh no, you are not going to go on about that" is a likely response to a university president who mentions the subject, but it is mentioned and repeated because it is unresolved and remains a serious problem – particularly for Canada's most research-intensive universities. Sometimes called the institutional costs of research, these are the costs that cannot be traced and attributed to a particular unit or research project: administrative and advisory services, insurance, and maintenance are common examples. Sometimes called hidden costs or overhead, they are estimated to add 40 per cent or more to the costs of research. Where universities enter into contracts for research, they can and do negotiate inclusion of indirect costs for full reimbursement or partial reimbursement if that is consistent with another interest in play in the negotiations. But in the case of research grants, and in particular those from NSERC, SSHRC, and CIHR, indirect costs are not included.

The 2003 federal budget included an indirect costs program to meet some of the costs associated with research sponsored by the Government of Canada. Now budgeted at $325 million, the global reimbursement rate is about 23 per cent. But because of the sliding scale calculation that provides a lower percentage of reimbursement for higher levels of research grant funding, the percentage reimbursement is lower for universities that achieve those higher levels of funding. For example, the University of Toronto's reimbursement rate is 18 per cent, far short of the indirect costs incurred by U of T in the high levels of granting council research conducted there.

The Canada Foundation for Innovation provides some indirect cost support for grants from its Infrastructure Operating Fund: 30 per cent of the CFI's contribution, but CFI contributes 40 per cent of full costs, which means it contributes 12 per cent of full indirect costs. Unless the recipient recovers additional indirect costs from other contributors, this means reimbursement for only a small portion of them.

In 2009, the Association of Universities and Colleges of Canada issued a discussion paper comparing treatment of indirect costs in Canada with their treatment in other countries, notably the United States, United Kingdom, European Union, and Australia. AUCC found that "where programs and policies are in place to meet institutional costs, universities are reimbursed at a much higher rate than in Canada – normally between 40 and 60 percent. The discrepancy is probably higher than it seems – in most cases and unlike in Canada – direct research grants cover faculty salaries; thus the institutional costs are calculated on a wider base."[64] At the time, Australia was an exception, but it has since announced a reimbursement rate of 50 per cent, to be achieved by 2014.[65]

The universities are not the only ones that should be interested in solving this problem. Provincial governments that pay much of the universities' operating costs should insist on a solution as well, because their contributions end up subsidizing the indirect costs of research as institutions in effect divert other monies to pay them. Students, too, should join the cause, again because some of their tuition payments are committed to this purpose. What is in effect a cross-subsidization by provincial governments and students of the indirect costs of federally sponsored research should be brought to an end.

Universities should be more insistent in bringing it to an end. Instead of being supplicants, going cap in hand to Ottawa to plead for a more robust program to federal officials who greet their plea with sighs of boredom, they should assert that indirect costs are part of doing federally sponsored research and must be paid. To do this they must act together, and at least the research-intensive U15 should be able to do so. Cumulatively they are influential, and the problem is more urgent for them because at present, and there is irony in this, they recover less of their indirect costs of research than do less-research-intensive universities.

With this problem, as with others, we greet the recurring theme of a need for greater coordination in the making of policy. The operating costs of major science infrastructure is a problem, but whose problem is it? The indirect costs of research is an issue, but whose issue is it? The answer is that they are everyone's and therefore no one's in particular, and so they are shuffled to the side to await the attention of another day. Again, no way to run a railroad, and no way to make Canadian science policy.

From gaps in science policy we should now turn our attention to translation and innovation. Tom Brzustowski is one to command our attention on the subject. He has served successively as professor of engineering, department chair and vice-president academic at University of Waterloo; deputy minister of Colleges and Universities and of the Premier's Council in Ontario; president of NSERC; and chair of the Scientific Advisory Committee of the Council of Canadian Academies. Most recently he has been a professor at University of Ottawa's Telfer School of Management. In his 2012 volume on innovation Brzustowski writes, "Some critics of the present system have said that Canada does not have an innovation policy; we have an invention policy. That statement is only half right. We certainly don't have an innovation policy; but we really don't have an invention policy either. We have a research policy. Invention is a challenging process on its own; it involves design, and it goes far beyond just using research results. A complete innovation policy must support all three key activities: research, design and commercialization wherever they are done, provided always that they meet high standards of quality as determined by appropriate measures."[66]

Brzustowski points to the importance of coordination as well. People moving through the phases of innovation – research, design, commercialization – and seeking government support "should be able to find it in the programs of one agency."[67]

Brzustowski calls for a Canadian innovation action plan. "This won't happen spontaneously," he writes, "it will take wise and strong leadership, hard work and persistence ... with buy-in from all orders of government in all regions, and from all sectors of the economy and of society ... To begin the process, a small group of the top leaders

of government and equal numbers of the acknowledged leading fig-
ures from business and from post-secondary education must jointly
develop a strategy for meeting that goal. The strategy must specify
who will do what and when. It must also create a transparent mechanism for receiving regular feedback on progress and making changes
in response to it.[68]

The Innovation Action Plan should have three goals: (1) private sector innovation that would raise the Canadian gross domestic product
per capita above "business as usual" numbers by 2 per cent a year,
and sustain this increase for a decade; (2) public sector innovation
"to update its institutions, systems and practices to meet the needs
of Canadians ... achieving increasing effectiveness and, at the same
time, improving efficiency in the use of resources";[69] and (3) focus of
all sectors on innovation to improve, protect, and preserve Canada's
environment.[70] While, as Brzustowski reminds us, "Innovation policy
doesn't produce innovations; entrepreneurs do that,"[71] a policy context
and climate that encourages innovation is needed.

Brzustowski asserts that lessons learned about innovation in our
country can be summarized in ten principles that should guide Canadian innovation policy (federal and provincial)[72] and nine program principles to guide implementation.[73] Cumulatively, the proposed action
plan, goals, and principles to guide innovation policy and programs
represent both an innovation landscape and a challenge to Canadians
comparable to those met in our greatest stories of nation-building. In
that our present policy shortcomings reflect the absence of either system or coordination, or both, a challenge of this magnitude is formidable but one worthy of our ambitions and energy.

The implications for universities begin with the second goal of calling
for public sector innovation to update institutions, systems, and practices to meet the needs of Canadians. Our universities are not exempt
from this appeal, and this book considers several areas in which they
can make updates and improvements in their ways: considered decisions about institutional positioning and differentiation; planning and
overcoming path dependency; improved capacity for partnerships
with government and industry; and improved governance and collegial management, together with an understanding of the role played
by a labour relations model ill-suited to self-governing institutions in a
post-industrial society.

Beyond updates to "institutions, systems and practices" are the
substantive connections of universities to innovation. Research is the

foundation, but it is the role universities have in linking research to invention and commercialization that makes them part of an innovation system. University research makes three contributions to innovation. "The first, which may be the most important in the long run but is the most difficult to predict, is the future work of the highly qualified people emerging from the system."[74] Solutions to industrial problems, and potential intellectual property that can lead to an invention licensed to an existing business or commercialized by a new one, are the second and third.[75] They require university-industry partnerships in project research, and a capacity to facilitate commercialization of inventions that might result from basic research.[76]

We saw in chapter 5 that universities have work to do to in order to become better partners. Greater openness to partnerships and more efficiency in their realization are required of many if not all of our universities. A university-industry partnership has its origins in a problem that requires new knowledge. A company formulates the problem and contacts a university that might be able to help, though with university business-development officers, as suggested by Wayne Brownlee,[77] it is possible the problem might be identified and formulated by a university as well as a company. If there is a good university-company fit, partnership follows, often with a detailed proposal for NSERC support to match the company's financial contribution. If the proposal is approved, the work begins. "Something very similar would occur in the NCE program, but in the broader context of a multi-company, multi-university network ... The research produces results and discoveries, and possibly also ideas for inventions. The results that contribute to the solution of the company's problem are transferred to the firm ... Discoveries are published in the open literature as new codified knowledge, possibly with a delay for competitive reasons."[78]

The potential for an invention may emerge from the partnership research project or from basic research. If the former, it will be subject to the intellectual property agreement that was part of the partnership agreement – typically assigned to the company for commercialization within the company or in a spin-off.[79] If the latter, we are reminded by Brzustowski that "inventions don't pop out of research results" and "may not always be the top-of-mind issue for researchers."[80] It often takes skilled and experienced people to recognize an invention, its possible design and market potential, and how to protect the intellectual property and to attract an entrepreneur to develop a business model.[81] There are some of these people in our universities now. More are needed.

If as Atkinson-Grosjean argues "Networks are becoming the default institutional structures in which public science is performed,"[82] *clusters* are key to private sector success and innovation. The contemporary usage of the word comes from Michael Porter and refers to a geographical concentration of people, talent, and resources connected in ways that give it sectoral or broader leadership in business and industry.[83] There are several in Canada; the National Research Council lists eleven cluster initiatives[84] and Brzustowski describes six actual clusters. My case study is one of them.

Several developments account for the agricultural biotechnology cluster in Saskatoon. The first had its origins in a university that was established in part to help build an industry. Agriculture was one of two foundational colleges at the University of Saskatchewan and the first such college in Canada to be established within a university rather than as a stand-alone school. The university's founders set aside nearly one thousand hectares for its main campus on which agricultural research has been a prominent activity and one that is visible, almost daily, to the city's residents and visitors. On nearly thirty hectares of this land sits Innovation Place, established in 1977 by a land lease with the university. Its ownership was vested in one crown corporation and later transferred to another, the Saskatchewan Opportunities Corporation, with a direct reporting relationship to the provincial government through the province's Crown Investments Corporation. Its mandate is to promote Saskatchewan's technology sector.

Science and technology parks are based on a simple concept. Bringing businesses with similar interests together in one place allows them to take advantage of network features and economies of scale. The physical grouping or clustering of organizations interested in innovation enhances productivity and success through interaction, collaboration, and the sharing of services and specialized infrastructure, the cost of which may be unaffordable to them individually.

Growth is important to clusters. Each addition to them increases the value of the whole. When the cluster reaches critical mass, it has self-sustaining momentum that leads to further growth, provided that growth is not precluded by extraneous factors.[85]

It takes a considered strategy to ensure that the concept of science and technology parks – growth and critical mass – is realized. Local, private technology companies are preferred tenants: they have the greatest potential for employment growth and loyalty to location. They are joined as highly desired clients by business and technical services organizations, research institutes, and national and global technology companies. Of importance are the right mix of technology and service clients; diversity achieved by attracting tenants that may be large or small, private or public, local or international; and facilities of high quality. Long-term commitment to sustainable buildings leads to good air quality, including minimal off-gassing from building materials, and access to daylight. The park's management responsibilities do not end there. The interaction of clients and the pace of networking must be supported by a program – social events, business seminars, and athletic competitions contribute to a growing sense of community. Fitness facilities, games rooms, yoga and Pilates classes all facilitate interaction. And good food helps: Boffins Club at Innovation Place is one of Saskatoon's finest dining establishments.

The strategy worked. In 2009 the Association of University Research Parks described Innovation Place as a leader in the global research community and named it the 2009 Outstanding Research Park.[86] In addition to a direct financial return of $10 million a year, the annual economic impact is $735 million, and most important, Saskatchewan has seventy-five technology companies that originated in Innovation Place.

The university's strength in agriculture and the 130 firms and nearly 3,500 jobs at Innovation Place were critical elements of this cluster. There were others. The Saskatoon research centre of Agriculture and Agrifoods Canada had a record that included Keith Downey's world-renowned work with rapeseed and canola;[87] NRC's Plant Biotechnology Institute, and a Bio Processing Centre added to the capacity and potential for this cluster. So too did the new global institutes for food and water security established in recent years at the U of S.

Other established clusters include aerospace in Montreal, photonics in Ottawa, life sciences in Toronto, digital media and ICT in Waterloo, and biotechnology in Vancouver. In addition, creative hubs like the MaRS Discovery District in Toronto, part of the life sciences cluster there, and Quartier De L'Innovation in Montreal offer great promise and models for the future. With examples and experience like this, the nascent eleven cluster initiatives named by NRC should enjoy success as well. These are success stories to be nurtured, imitated, and celebrated.

In summary, Canadians carry considerable advantages into the globally competitive world of innovation. We do good science; we know our weaknesses as well as our strengths. We have fine examples of innovation success. We have potential for much more. But we have disadvantages to overcome: we remain under-performers in knowledge

translation and innovation. The federal government's shift in emphasis
to excellence described in chapter 1 was not accompanied by the kind
of national initiative described by Brzustowski – an innovation action
plan – to locate the new emphasis within a broader strategic context.
The NCEs might have been a component of that new context, but they
were not a substitute for it.

It is difficult to mobilize our big and sometimes awkward country
behind bold ambition. Apart from our decentralized federation, politicians and those they serve are understandably wary of big goals. We
anticipate or fear falling short, and a major discrepancy between ambition and achievement is no better for countries than it is for people.
And so we remain incrementalists, and even our incrementalism has
not been planned, coordinated, or even informed by leading thinkers
on innovation. This must change – and soon.

We Canadians are good self-analysts. On science, technology, and
related matters such as competition and productivity we have produced
report after report that cumulatively reinforce our strengths while failing to generate the concerted effort and plan needed to overcome our
well-documented weaknesses. It is not beyond us to do so. There are
periods in our history when Canadians, including those who lead them,
have responded superbly to the imperatives of nation-building. This is
another such period, and we need to be summoned once again to build
Canada, this time through innovation.

Chapter Eight

Leadership with an Asterisk: On the Precarious Presidency

Among the final items on the agenda for meetings of the board of governors is an in-camera meeting without its president. This meeting is enough to inspire curiosity and sometimes anxiety in the president, and the longer the meeting, the greater the curiosity and the more likely it becomes anxiety. Whatever the board members are talking about, you know that it involves you, and they are saying things they prefer to say in your absence. These meetings are necessary for good governance, because they encourage disclosure and candour among board members, and they prepare the board chair to have informal and frank conversations with the president. If there are signals or even warnings about presidential performance, they are likely to arise and be discussed in this way – at least they should be.

I was in my office as an in-camera meeting progressed, and it was a long one. Upon its conclusion the chair and vice-chair made their way into my office, closed the door behind them, and sat down, facing me across my conference table. They were serious and deliberate. The board chair began, "Members of the board believe you to be an optimist," he said. "We wonder if you have people around you who present a more guarded picture, pointing to risks as well as benefits." I thought carefully before replying: "Would you like me to appoint a vice-president of pessimism?"

The board's concern was understandable. A positive attitude and demeanour is part of the mental equipment of university presidents; a solemn and negative one is a virtual disqualification for the office. But presidents must also see their world as it is. They must appraise their universities' circumstances in real terms, and they must understand their weaknesses and threats as well as strengths and opportunities.

In asserting that "the task of leadership is to make vision practical and compelling,"[1] Bart Giamatti was conveying the idea that vision must be informed by what is possible in addition to bold ambition. And what is possible is influenced in part by the difficulty of altering the institution's current path or status quo. But sometimes that is what leadership is for: raising sights and altering direction, and this cannot be done without optimism, if not about present circumstances, at least about future prospects.

Never has Canadian university presidential leadership been under greater scrutiny than it is today. The contemporary volume on the subject is called *Leadership under Fire*.[2] Peter Drucker describes a university presidency as the hardest job in modern society,[3] and the *Globe and Mail*'s Jeffrey Simpson wrote, "Apart from the resident of 24 Sussex Drive, the ladies and gentlemen who run Canada's universities have the country's toughest job."[4] "Universities are terribly difficult to manage. There are boards, senates, faculty associations, unions, alumni, the gridlock of tenure, student politics, town-gown relations, dealings with governments and, often, very tight budgets."[5]

Whether the job is hard, harder, or hardest, there is empirical evidence of the risk one assumes in taking on the role. Former University of Victoria president David Turpin has documented the steady decline in length of Canadian presidential service, as well as the unprecedented number of early departures on account of dismissals, pressured exits, or early resignations.[6] In the past decade, approximately twenty presidencies in the ninety-seven Canadian universities have ended this way, causing personal and professional damage to the individuals involved as well as significant disruption and cost to the universities from whose presidential offices they parted. Superficial exploration of reasons yields common explanations – "He was not a fit," "We didn't warm to her," "He wasn't one of us," "She clashed with the board" (or faculty, or students, or whomever). A more searching investigation reveals underlying reasons with greater clarity. The modern university presidency has spheres of activity, numbers of constituencies, and diffusion of authority that make for ambiguity in defining the role, determining its responsibilities, and measuring success. This concept of the office was captured by a distinguished president of two leading American universities who wrote,

I manage to serve this organization as part figurehead, part pastor of interpersonal relations, part spokesperson, part disburser of institutional propaganda and positive reinforcement to students, faculty, alumni and trustees; I manage to be an unprincipled (at times) promoter and princi-pled (at other times) huckster of the institution and its objectives. I manage to bring forward the historical traditions of the institution and give some of them new life and meaning in a different world; I manage to articulate a set of goals for the institution that, despite all odds, actually covers all the activities of what increasingly has become a general-service-public utility; I manage an organization of bewildering scope.[7]

Managing this "organization of bewildering scope" is complicated by internal structures that at their best constitute a system of checks and balances, and at their worst can be obstructive to change, even paralytic. And yet a president today is expected, externally at least, to "get the university's act together" – to manage, not merely to broker different interests, contain others, check intrusions, and produce calm. A president is expected to have the opportunity as well as the capacity to make a difference for the better. Yet leading Canadian presidents, when asked by Ross Paul whether they can make a difference,[8] offer guarded responses: "Not much," said former UBC president Martha Piper, who believes leaders in general can make a difference but is not confident that university leaders share that opportunity.[9] Former Queen's principal Bill Leggett commented upon "the ephemeral qual-ity of many achievements"[10] and was guarded about the potential for enduring change.[11] Carleton's Roseann Runte no doubt expressed the experience of many in saying, "You have to wait sometimes until peo-ple are ready for change – you have to slow down and back up a bit."[12] Rob Pritchard (Toronto), Jim Downey (UNB, Carleton, Waterloo), and David Marshall (Nipissing, Mount Royal) were confident that presi-dents make a difference, though imprecise about the difference they make. Setting the institution's tone (Downey),[13] nurturing its climate (Horowitz),[14] and the influence of voice (Davenport)[15] were cited as important positive differences they can make. Bonnie Patterson (Trent) adds, "I don't know how to measure how much difference a president makes, but without the leadership and vision and the will to get imple-mentation, I think you would have either a petrified campus where nothing would change or you would have a floundering one, all over the place."[16]

Leadership, yes, but with an asterisk that represents hesitancy about its scope and impact. Consider, for example, the challenge presented by results-based management. In the not-so-distant past, a president "was more apt to 'preside over' than to lead or manage the institution."[17] Presiding is about moderating and sometimes guiding, as distinct from steering and – occasionally – determining, and it presumes little or nothing about a university's comparable performance and results, let alone accountability for them. But that is not the world of today's university president. If the university is among the best, its president is expected to keep it there or even to improve its standing among the select institutions to which it seeks to be compared. If a university is not among the best, its board and external constituencies are or should be interested in knowing its plans for improvement, and for this they will look to the president. This change in expectations raises a prominent theme in today's university discourse, that of corporatization.

> "Corporatization" of universities is an idea that has been much discussed and written about in academic circles in recent years, both in Canada and more generally ... The very fact that the new "good governance" practices originated in the corporate world, and that it is the external members of university boards of governors who have urged their use, may have been seen as reasons to resist their incursion into the academy. This resistance may also be exacerbated by the language of stakeholders and shareholders, corporations, directors and customers to be found in the various instruments and templates that abound in the world of corporate governance.[18]

Designating and describing university presidents as chief executive officers is part of this idea, and it too meets resistance, because it is seen as attributing to them powers comparable to those held by their corporate counterparts. The unique governance and collegial management of universities means that their presidents do not have the same powers – a fact not always understood by those outside the university, and some from within, who look to the president for many things, including accountability for results. For as long as the results were seen only as keeping the doors open and the finances in order, this did not exert undue pressure on them. But this is no longer the case. The performance of universities is being measured and will continue to be measured. The process of differentiation in quality is no longer subtle and impressionistic; it is one of numbers, rankings, and surveys, and it is public. While it is true that the measures cannot account for all, they can account for much, and they are influential. The public reads them, and so do government leaders and members of boards of governors.

They want to know what they mean, and what they imply about the future – and they want to know what is being done about them.

The theme of path dependency has already been introduced in this volume.[19] The idea is not only that once a trajectory – good or otherwise – is established, it tends to be followed (history matters), but rather that deviation from an established path is unlikely because there are positive reinforcements for it along the way. Resistance to change in its various manifestations is among these positive reinforcements. "Things are fine as they are"; "We are better than numbers, and surveys say we are"; "The numbers don't matter because we are different": these are the rationalizations of positive reinforcement for a status quo, for an established path not to be disrupted, and for avoiding accountability for results.

We have thus come to one of the principal reasons why the modern university presidency is precarious: presidents increasingly are held to account for results over which they have little control. If they protest, citing the limits of their authority, they are rightly met with the reply that if they don't control the results, they must hold to account those who do. In other words, universities as a whole must be answerable for their performance and standing, and if they are not presently organized so as to provide that accountability, organizational change is necessary to enable them to do so.

The process of organizational change brings university presidents who embark upon it into conflict with the self-reinforcing mechanisms of path dependency and a status quo that has more leverage to avoid change than is found in other organizations. The ensuing struggles, though necessary, are predictable and severe. The array mustered in resistance is substantial. It includes those in denial of a new and explicitly competitive university world; those who make over-broad claims in the name of academic freedom; those who are ideologically disposed to the status quo because they see change in the name of accountability as corporatization; and faculty unions reinforced by their national organization, the Canadian Association of University Teachers. It is no wonder that the fight tests the endurance of university presidents.

Being accountable for matters beyond one's control, combined with a struggle for organizational change to effect greater accountability, is not the only explanation for the precariousness of the modern university presidency. The lack of preparation and mentorship for the role, and institutional weaknesses in succession planning, are others. With respect to the first of these, there is in the academy a deep suspicion of ambition to occupy high administrative office: everyone should want to be a full professor but no one should want to be president. A virtually certain disqualification for a presidency is reserved for those who appear to want it more than they should; better to appear a reluctant suitor dragged to the altar than to be the first to arrive at the church.

On one level this is understandable. Explicit interest in and pursuit of high office leads to a concern that the office is sought more for its own sake than for the positive things that can be achieved by its occupant. The cost is that there are no heirs apparent who are being prepared to serve as presidents – at least not at their present institutions. Compare this with industry, where future CEOs are often current chief operating officers being groomed at the side of the CEO for the corner office, or with the public service where a career progression to senior executive positions is understood and encouraged. There remains in the university world a romantic attachment to the idea that the academy reaches into an academic department to second a professor reluctantly willing to put on hold her fine academic career so as to serve for a short time as president before returning to her academic work a few years later. The time for this idea, if ever there was one, has long since passed, but its influence persists in the reluctance to engage in succession planning. The consequence is that many who arrive in a president's office have insufficient preparation for the magnitude of the job that lies before them. Most adjust to it in time; others fall early victims to the precarious presidency. But for all there is a steep and time consuming learning curve.

The reluctance to engage in succession planning means that a sitting president cannot groom and mentor an internal successor. She has little or no influence in identifying who will follow her in the office, and presidential search committees have a strong bias in favour of external candidates.[20] And given that bias, most new presidents of Canadian universities must learn on the job as they are becoming familiar with a new institution and a new home. It is a heavy burden.

Paul Davenport observes, "I think the reason that the outgoing president is not at all involved in the selection of the successor, which is the case at every university I know, is so the new president can have this immaculate conception aura around him or her."[21] If this is the reason, it is not a sound one. The new president – like all the old ones – is appointed, not anointed, and a positive aura does not last for long. An aura that passes quickly is a steep price to pay for the absence of preparation for the job.

In the United States, as in Canada, university and college presidencies can be precarious. "During 2009 and 2010, fifty college, university and system presidents resigned, retired prematurely, or were fired."[22] In *Presidencies Derailed*[23] Stephen Trachtenberg, Gerald Kauvar, and Grady Bogue explore the reasons for these failures in leadership. They observe that "three underlying and often overlapping factors can undo a presidency."[24] The first is personal shortcomings (unethical behaviour, stubbornness, poor interpersonal skills, and ineffective communication styles). Failure to understand or adjust to the features, cultures, and idiosyncrasies of an institution is another. A third is board shortcomings. "In some derailments, the board is as much a part of the problem as the president. Leadership of academic institutions depends on good governance and a productive board–president relationship. Some presidents fall victim to flawed search processes. Others discover pre-existing conditions of board dysfunction, such as micromanagement, weak oversight, or internal schisms. A few stumble into unethical and disheartening board behaviour, such as breaches of confidentiality and conflicts of interest."[25]

Personal shortcomings, adjustment problems and board weaknesses are not new. Early departures of so many presidents suggests either that universities have not learned from past leadership failures, or they are more reluctant to live with them until a graceful exit can be arranged. The answer may lie in both.

The Americans have devoted considerable attention to the modern university/college presidency. In 2006 a seventeen-member task force reported on its state,[26] the second time in a decade that such an effort had been mounted. In 1996 the Association of Governing Boards of Universities and Colleges released a report, the gist of which was that these institutions needed "to free themselves from processes of excessive internal consultation – in effect, to empower presidents to be purposeful decision makers."[27] The 2006 report observed, "At the outset of the 21st century, colleges and universities face an array of daunting challenges. To name a few: intense global competition, rapid technological advancements, changing demographics, increased demand for education and training, new ways of delivering instruction, greater pressures for accountability, and inadequate funding to achieve societal purposes. Facing these challenges is critical to creating the human and intellectual capital to ensure the nation's continued social, civic and economic well-being. America's higher education institutions must be the engines of society's transformation."[28]

And presidents are critical to the success of this mission: "No leader comes to personify an institution in the way a president does. A president must provide leadership in maintaining the institution's academic integrity and reputation. He or she must assimilate and tell the institution's story to build pride internally and support externally. The president has primary responsibility for increasing public understanding and support for the institution as a contributor to the nation's continued vitality and well-being, and must lead the institution as it confronts new external challenges."[29]

The task force found that "colleges and universities continue to face impediments in their efforts to achieve effective governance and sustain capable leadership."[30] These impediments "are traceable to the intensity and range of conflicting pressures a president must confront – and from the fact that presidents receive uneven guidance, support and oversight from their governing boards."[31] Put in stark terms, there is a gap between the demands of the job and the capacity of the institutions to deliver on the conditions necessary to enable its successful performance. This is a fundamental problem, and it has several dimensions. The task force did what a body commissioned by an association of governing boards could; it focused on the relationship between presidents and boards, though its recommendations have broader import. They provide a useful framework for a discussion of these issues in Canada, as they do in the United States.

The task force asserts that in the modern university the compelling need is for integral leadership. "Leadership of this sort links the president, the faculty and the board together in a well-functioning partnership purposefully devoted to a well-defined, broadly affirmed institutional vision. Such leadership successfully engages the faculty, student leaders and key external stakeholders in achieving collectively what no single individual or unit can accomplish individually. Finally, integral leadership is characterized by integrity – by a capacity for reasoned judgment, fairness, and a commitment to the core values and mission of the institution."[32]

We should now review the implications of this concept of leadership for boards and for other parts of the university community. For boards, the essentials are to establish clear expectations and to ensure that the president assimilates the institutional culture, builds a leadership team, and develops a strategic plan. The board must also present a unified stand in support of the president on contentious issues and must avoid injecting personal agendas or otherwise meddling in operations.[33] Of course the key here is confidence. The board must have confidence in the president's capacity for integral leadership, and this confidence originates with the presidential search.

Widely acknowledged to be its single most important task, a board often has less influence in a presidential appointment than might be expected. In part this is because the presidential search is not conducted by the board or even by a committee of the board, but by a committee with board members in addition to faculty, students, and sometimes others chosen by alumni, professional staff, and unions. The advantage of this broadly based committee is that it reflects university constituents and gives them voice in a process that is important to the acceptance and credibility of their chosen candidate. The disadvantage is that acceptability to a constituency base may outweigh other considerations as a presidential search develops and matures. This is not explicit, of course, but the opportunity afforded by membership on a search committee to influence choice based on constituency interests should not be underestimated. Idiosyncratic perspectives and informal networks of communication within and among the people who staff universities can have powerful influence in university searches – not only for presidents, but for other administrative officers and faculty. This is particularly so when committee members from the same constituency – say faculty or students – caucus or communicate among themselves outside of committee deliberations, drawing upon sources of information that are not shared with others on the committee.

Boards and search committees can take measures to reduce these risks from materializing. A board should ensure that its understanding of the university's circumstances and prospects is accepted by a search committee from the outset, and it should remind the committee that it is the board's responsibility and not the committee's to make the appointment. The difference between appointing and rubber-stamping is not always clear and simple. A board can be put in a position where its members feel that they have little choice but to accept a recommendation from a search committee, and they may be right. If the board has not been clear about its expectations from the beginning of the search, or if it is not insistent about an assessment of a candidate against those expectations, it may have de facto forfeited its responsibility to make the appointment.

The retention of professional search consultants has become a common feature of presidential searches. These are people who can help identify prospective candidates, persuade good prospects to allow their names to be considered, develop and refine a position profile, and conduct reference checks. They can also advise and assist the chair of the search committee, who is unlikely to have previously been involved in the unique processes of a search of this kind. Confined to their proper role, search consultants can be invaluable for their connections, advice, and services. But in the United States, and it can be surmised in Canada too, there can be "excessive reliance on a presidential search consultant to carry out the board's own responsibilities ... Too often ... the board and its search committee cede the very choice of a president to a consultant. Excessive deference to a consultant's presumed expertise can undermine the integrity of a search process. The final decision must reflect the judgment of the board and its search committee – as opposed to a consultant, who may be as concerned with advancing a specific set of candidates as with identifying a candidate well suited to the institution's needs."[34]

There can also be excessive reliance upon the interview stage of the search process. Paul observes that "interviews are notoriously unreliable,"[35] a judgment that recognizes the subjectivity of the exercise as well as the tendency of search committees to fall in love with external candidates about whom little is known apart from virtuoso interview performances. But Paul's caution is often unheeded in a process geared to the identification of a pool of three or four candidates to be invited by the committee to undergo an interview. The ultimate or penultimate stage of the process consists of the interviews themselves, usually conducted in a short period so that they can be compared by the committee. The identification of a preferred candidate usually follows shortly, thus reinforcing a sense that interviews are the most influential factors in the final decision.

"A candidate's previous performance in leadership positions is ... the best predictor of ability to perform a new job and one that is considerably more reliable than the average interview."[36] Systematic, detailed, and deep background checks are of great importance, and no presidential appointment should be made without them. Boards should take measures to ensure that they are accorded the weight they merit in presidential searches, and that they are not overshadowed by evidence – including interviews – that may be less reliable.

The selection of a president-designate is the beginning rather than the end of the work of both search committee and board. The members of the former must remain engaged so as to assist in transition; the latter must settle upon a presidential contract and help prepare for the assumption of office by the new president. In recent years contracts have become public documents, and the terms and conditions of employment are known within and beyond the university community. Predictably, attention is most immediately drawn to compensation. "A president's compensation should be linked to achievement of agreed upon performance goals as measured through a regular process of evaluation, and compensation should be indexed to appropriate standards of reference within and outside of the institution – including comparisons with peer institutions."[37]

The "appropriate standards of reference" will be debated, of course, and sometimes highly publicized and criticized. The starting point for many will be a comparison of public and private sector compensation. "Studies show that public-sector workers are overcompensated compared to workers who do the 'same' jobs in the private sector. Research published by the Fraser Institute in April, 2013, for instance, showed a 12% gap, confirming earlier studies by the Montreal Economic Institute, C.D. Howe, and others."[38]

Precisely the opposite is the case in executive salary and benefits. "The compensation of most college and university presidents is far less than that of the chief executives of comparable for-profit enterprises."[39] No one is suggesting it should be otherwise. Most universities and colleges are public institutions, and it is the public sector that provides the context. But these are very senior public sector jobs and they are appropriately compared to presidencies of crown corporations, large health boards and hospitals, and deputy ministers in government.

What is important is not the fact of controversy over pay and benefits. Controversy is inevitable, because it is human nature to compare compensation and to make judgments, however wise or informed, on the subject. The question that must be asked is one of policy because, like other public sector employers, universities must have defensible compensation policies.

In my early years at the University of Saskatchewan, executive compensation for academic leaders (president, vice-presidents, deans) was not competitive. There was a grudging acceptance or even a perverse pride that this had to be so: Saskatchewan could not compete in the recruitment of executive talent; we grew our own and they had to be content with their lot. As president I understood the negative consequences of this attitude and asked the board of governors to approve a compensation policy for all academic personnel, from assistant professor to president. By this policy we would track salaries at seven other universities: Alberta, Calgary, Manitoba, Guelph, McMaster, Western, and Dalhousie. The first three were the other prairie medical-doctoral universities; Guelph, like the University of Saskatchewan, had faculties of agriculture and veterinary medicine; McMaster, Western, and Dalhousie were other medical-doctoral schools of roughly comparable size and were included to add a broader, national perspective. In a period of intense competition for academic talent, the U of S would expect neither to lead nor to trail this group but to be at about the seventy-fifth percentile in the salaries we offered. The board approved the policy and our competitive position improved greatly.

Leaves of absence are another controversial element of compensation for academic personnel. Professors are eligible for paid leave for research purposes for one year out of seven; academic administrative personnel are often eligible for leave, for research or retooling purposes, after five years in an administrative post. These leaves are not paid vacations, they are and should be monitored to ensure they are used for the intended purposes. In my own case, because I was in administration for twenty-three of my thirty-seven years at the University of Saskatchewan, I did not take three of the leaves for which I was eligible, because they would have disrupted the continuing administrative work for which I was responsible. I undertook to write this book in a leave after my presidential term.

There are other terms common in presidential contracts that can exacerbate the precarious presidency. Initial terms are usually for five years, but some boards seek to include a term in the contract that provides for termination without cause on short notice. In effect this means that a new president who signs a contract containing such a provision makes a five-year commitment to her institution, while the board is committed only until it decides otherwise. Of course boards do not want to end presidencies prematurely, but it should not be easy for them to do so in the absence of good and sufficient cause. New presidents should resist signing contracts containing such a provision.

Once there is a new president with a signed contract, the board must maintain oversight of his work. "To obtain the best possible return on a board's investment in presidential talent and compensation, the board should establish a process for providing meaningful feedback on its assessment of the president's performance. For both the institution and the president, regular feedback offers a gauge of performance as well as an opportunity to celebrate success ... A board strengthens a presidency by offering constructive feedback at regular intervals."[40]

And yet discussions with some of the presidents who left office unwillingly and in substantial numbers in the past decade suggest that many Canadian boards need to improve these processes. In a surprising number of cases, presidents who have been dismissed were unaware of their peril until their departures were imminent. In some cases, board chairs were passive in the face of mounting difficulties or were instrumental in a rising tide against an incumbent president. These are the people who are supposed to provide feedback, advice, and timely warning when necessary. When they do not do so, they fail both the president and the university.

The precarious presidency is further reflected in its timed phases. Considering that most presidents are new to their institutions; that they are unlikely to have received preparation or mentorship for the role and must learn on the job; that their boards are at best uneven in their expectations and feedback; and that universities are slow to adapt to new leadership, the initial university judgment on their performance arrives quickly. Most contracts are for five years, with reviews for potential renewal in the penultimate or fourth year, which means that the review begins some months after the end of year three. A committee – often identical or similar to a search committee – is struck and tasked with deciding whether to recommend that the president continue in office.

There is an advantage to this fourth-year judgment. It can provide a gracious exit where either university or president concludes that a mistake was made, or that circumstances have changed (perhaps the president's health has deteriorated) in ways that suggest departure is advisable. For purposes of assessing a president's substantive achievements, however, it is too early. The most that can be determined is that there has been a promising beginning – or otherwise.

Assuming reappointment, a Canadian university president can reasonably be assured of an opportunity to serve for ten years. Only a few serve more; the majority serve less. "For example, for those Ontario presidents who completed their first term in the past 20 years, the average length of service was 8.4 years. The situation would be similar in most universities in other provinces, although there are one or two institutions with a history of high turnover at certain periods in their history."[41] There are several reasons for durations of service that are sharply reduced over those of earlier years. The universities are orders of magnitude larger and more complex than in earlier years, and the burdens of office are correspondingly greater; some universities have policies and practices that discourage more than two terms in office;

and university communities grow tired of their presidents. An American survey "found that presidents were supported by 75 percent of faculty members in the first three years of their term of office but by only 25 percent when they were more than five years into the job."[42]

In short, a president who has been intensely recruited and hailed as a new leader more often than not is gone within ten years, frequently much earlier. For some, this may be a good thing, while for others it may be excessively high turnover. What it does mean, however, is that a president has one opportunity only to effect real change in a university's trajectory and promise. The early learning curve, developing a plan and persuading the university's many communities of its merits, the beginnings of implementation and perhaps early measurements of progress – by this stage, a president is closer to the end of her time in office than to the beginning. Certainly there is not time for going in one direction, determining that it is inadvisable, reversing course, and starting again. The precarious presidency offers only one chance to make a real difference.

Whether to strengthen the precarious presidency, and how to do so, remain outstanding questions. This book is about public policy, and so we should be clear that the questions are ones of policy and not of individual or constituency interests or preferences. Is it in the public interest to strengthen the senior leadership of our public universities? Our answer to this question must be informed by what we expect from this leadership in the twenty-first century.

We should begin by recalling the observation of Harvard's Derek Bok that "the strongest universities tend to perpetuate themselves virtually automatically."[43] He was speaking of the benefits to universities that have established reputations and lots of money, but his words have wider import. Established reputation and money don't materialize out of thin air. The former is established and sustained by a commitment to excellence reflected in the quality of academic appointments and by conditions enabling their success. And with success comes money, whether from granting councils, foundations, partners, or philanthropists. The significance of Bok's point is that quality is self-reinforcing through the standards, cultures, and supports of the university. Harvard expects its academic departments to be among the best in the world, and it expects its faculty and academic leadership to keep them there.

Bok's point has broader application within universities. They are not uniformly excellent. The bigger ones have many academic units – departments, faculties, schools, and colleges – of variable quality, and the variations may be considerable. Within the same university the natural sciences may be stronger than the social sciences, or the history department may be much better than languages. The expectations that faculty and academic leadership have of themselves are different in good departments from those in weaker ones.

The force of Bok's point is felt when we take licence to extend it to acknowledging that universities of variable or lesser quality also "tend to perpetuate themselves virtually automatically." Their standards, cultures, practices, and supports reinforce their current state and stature. An inference, of course, is that there is little that presidents can do about it: if you are good you are good; if you are not, you are not – self-satisfaction or fatalism depending on where you sit. But university presidents are not appointed to indulge in self-satisfaction or fatalism. They are expected to lead in making the mediocre better, the good very good, the very good excellent, and the excellent pre-eminent. And depending upon the magnitude of the task, they are expected to disrupt, modify, or adjust their universities' established paths. If this is an accurate statement of the expectations and responsibilities of presidential leadership, what are its implications for the authority we should vest in them, the qualities they should bring to the office, and the ways in which we identify and prepare them for their duties?

Our consideration of these questions must begin with a brief reference to the work of universities. The most important determinant of success in the academic world is the quality of the faculty and academic administration. In multiversities, the amount and quality of research determines ranking and reputation, and they in turn attract students at home and abroad. In other universities they may not receive the same emphasis as in research-intensive schools, but it is important nonetheless. Universities are alone among educational institutions in having and declaring a duty to produce new knowledge. Demonstrable success in research is an essential component of both successful universities and flourishing academic careers.

No little ink has been spilled in debates about the relationship between research and teaching, or on the undeniable importance of the latter. The lack of established and common measures of teaching evaluation means that rankings do not take account of variable teaching success across institutions as they do differential research achievement. But the quality of teaching should be and is important to academic career success, and to a university's reputation. However, apart from relatively new academic position streams representing a teaching-only commitment, faculty members are expected to demonstrate strength in both teaching and research, and their time in the classroom is such that they should have protected time for the latter. Apart from limited exceptions, it is not open to a university professor to disclaim interest in either teaching or research, or to avoid demonstrating a required standard of competence in both.

Service is the third dimension in the triumvirate of university duties, and it is defined in sufficiently general terms to include service within and beyond an academic unit, and within or outside the university itself. Faculty are expected to serve on committees and to be available for other internal or external engagements. There is little by way of prescription in the distribution of service responsibilities, and academic personnel are accorded considerable discretion in determining how they will discharge this duty.

The president's job is to build a team that can do this work to the highest possible standards. Of course she inherits a team and so does not build it from the start, unless her institution is a new one. Supporting her in this mission of teaching, research, and service are department heads, deans, provosts, and vice-presidents academic, and their assistants and associates. All universities have collegial processes for the identification of potential candidates for these offices, and questions arise as to the role of the president in relation to them. The idea that presidents must at least have voice, and sometimes the decisive voice, in selecting others in academic leadership positions is contested by some, particularly faculty unions, many of which have had success through collective bargaining in excluding presidents from these decisions or sharply curtailing their roles in them.

Obviously presidents cannot be personally involved in all or most of these search and appointment processes. But they or their offices, particularly through provosts, must be connected to some of them. Let us consider four areas in which their engagement is necessary, beginning with the senior executive group. Variously described as the president's executive, cabinet (in the United States), or senior management team, these are the people who work most closely with a president, and their offices are extensions of his. They include all vice-presidents and often senior board officers such as university secretaries. They may include others whose regular presence at executive meetings is thought to be desirable. Widely acknowledged to be the most senior among them is the provost, who is the day-to-day leader of the academic community. Typically presidents will chair search committees for these offices and must concur in any appointment to them. They are the senior team, and a president must have the decisive voice in determining team membership.

In particular academic units, deans are what the president is in the university as a whole – the leaders of their faculties, colleges, or schools – and they have responsibility for their academic and financial affairs. Having outstanding deans is critical to the success of the university and its academic units, and their appointments are usually made by boards on recommendation of presidents. But here the authority of presidents' offices may be contested. In some universities and academic units a culture has developed that views the appointment of a dean as a de facto prerogative of the unit which she is to lead; a president's or provost's duty is to seek the board's approval for the candidate preferred by a majority on the search committee. But what happens if the committee is sharply divided or a bare majority points to a conclusion with which the provost and president cannot agree?

The situation is not hypothetical. Decanal search committees may include faculty and students in numbers that can carry the day in a straight vote. They are not always motivated by identifying the person with the best qualifications for the position; they may want an acceptable insider, or someone who will not rock the boat. If in addition they see themselves as delegates of faculty and students whose views they must reflect in committee deliberations and votes, they in effect operate as a caucus within the search committee, thereby sidelining committee members from outside the academic unit.

A board's authority to appoint deans on the recommendation of president and provost is not a formality for the rubber-stamping of a bare majority view on a search committee. Universities need excellent leadership from their deans, and it is the responsibility of the senior administration to ensure that they get it. Presidents and provosts must have three choices in receiving the results of a search committee's deliberations: endorse a recommended candidate, declare a failed search and launch a new one, or recommend to the board another candidate who had support in the search committee but who was not supported by the majority. Fortunately, most of the time the first option is available and appropriate and is the one taken. But options two and three must be available if the evolution of the search points to them as necessary.

Department heads present a more complicated case. On one hand, their leadership is very important to the success of their departments; on the other, their position within universities is ambiguous. They have managerial responsibilities, but they are typically seen as aligned more with their departments than with the university. Their offices are in the department; the self-reinforcing voices are those of the faculty and students whom they see often. If the faculty are unionized, they are often included within the bargaining unit and are union members. In addition, they are not seen as having opted for a career in administration; they are more likely to be considered past and future members of the department who have agreed – often reluctantly – to assume the added burdens of the department chair for a few years. Cumulatively these circumstances can lead department heads to take a more limited view of their responsibilities than they should. They may be reluctant to act at variance with what are viewed as departmental prerogatives and preferences and as a result may be inclined to avoid difficult decisions that can bring criticism or a decline in popularity. This may be so, particularly in tenure matters where a department head may share his department's reluctance to make a negative recommendation for a congenial colleague who falls short of the required standard.

The status of the department head requires reconsideration, at least in some universities. To begin with, if their university faculty is unionized, they should be excluded from membership for the duration of their headship. They have management responsibilities that are incompatible with union status. This would also free the university to offer recompense commensurate with their responsibilities. Large departments may have more faculty than some units headed by deans, and their administrative responsibilities occupy most of their time on the job. They should be recognized and rewarded for what they are: leaders and managers. As such, they should not be chosen by those for whom they have management responsibilities but by those with whom they share them. This does not preclude weight attached to preferences of departmental faculty. It means simply that these preferences should not be binding. Deans to whom heads report should have the final say, and in exercising it, they should be confident that the provost shares their views about the kind of leadership required in the department concerned.

Permanent appointments to faculty are also a special case. Historically the authority of presidents in this respect was uncontested. It was understood that the single most important decision in the development of new universities was the appointment of its faculty and enabling legislation provided for presidential and board leadership in this area.[44] As small universities became big ones, the personal engagement of presidents became more remote, but governance legislation and regulation continued to recognize the fundamental importance of academic appointments and insisted on presidential responsibility for them. Recall, for example, that the modern version (1995) of the University of Saskatchewan Act provides that the president shall make recommendations to the board respecting the appointment, promotion, or removal of any faculty member.[45] The stature attributed to these appointments (in no other employment setting would you find the subject addressed in legislation) is inseparable from the fact that these are not ordinary jobs. The awarding of tenure is a career-long commitment of the university to the professor. Short of professional misconduct, it is unlikely that tenure will be interrupted or ended. The investment by a university in each tenured faculty member is a multi-million-dollar one and it should not be made except with the greatest care and confidence, and where multi-million-dollar investments are concerned, it should be expected that boards of governors and their senior administrations are involved and bear ultimate responsibility for them.

But one of the most signal – and negative – developments in recent years has been the delegation, in collective agreements, of tenure decisions to academic units operating under procedures that sometimes represent a lowest-common-denominator approach to the decision. I have witnessed this not once or twice but on many occasions, and I am confident that the experience is not unique to my university. My efforts to bring an end to the situation are still before courts and arbitrators.[46]

Excellent university departments usually uphold high standards in their tenure deliberations, though the standards they represent can be frustrated by appeal processes that revert to a lower standard. And when left to individual units, standards may vary according to the academic quality and rigour of the departments. This is why there must be insistence that university standards – not departmental ones or those of individual faculties – provide the benchmark. And where university standards are the benchmark, it is the university's administration that must assure the board that they are of sufficient rigour, and that they are being honoured in the board's multi-million-dollar investment in each faculty member.

The capacity of presidents to lead their universities is what provoked this excursus into appointment matters, and it is to that capacity that we now return. The main point should be clear: if university presidents are to provide the leadership they are expected to provide in the twenty-first century, they must have, maintain, or recover – as the case may be – its single most important lever, what shapes its talent pool. The case is clear with members of the senior executive team and university deans. The president must have the capacity to choose the former and to be influential in choosing the latter. Provosts and deans must be influential in the selection of department heads and must ensure that presidents are aligned with their thinking. And presidents must exercise rather than delegate or concede their authority to make recommendations to the board on awards of tenure. These are multi-million-dollar investments by universities, and it is part of the board's fiduciary responsibility to be satisfied on the advice of its senior executive that every such investment is a good one.

Left to one side in the discussion thus far is the question about the merits of tenure itself. It is a deeply entrenched feature of university life supported by an assumption that it remains an essential protection of academic freedom. Yet its meaning is fuzzy, its context has changed, and it has become invested with a mythical status to mean employment until voluntary retirement or death, terminable only by gross neglect or misbehaviour. Context here is particularly important. Tenure for university faculty first appeared in a world without the contractual, employment law, and human rights protections available today. Added to these in Canada is an end to mandatory retirement, which, considering modern life expectancies, can mean tenured careers of forty years or more. The question is fairly asked and renewed, whether tenure serves an important public policy purpose in Canada in the twenty-first century.

It is important that this question be answered by universities themselves. The precise meaning of tenure varies among them, and its continuance is an employment matter to be resolved internally, bearing in mind the new context referenced above. However, it is fair to add that the support of public institutions rests on confidence in their purpose, governance, and operations, and that tenure has acquired a status such that it must be demonstrably justified in order to sustain this support. The case has not yet been made.

Clarification and where necessary recovery of the leverage that shapes the talent pool is perhaps the most important area of presidential authority that requires attention, if we are to narrow the gap between expectations of presidential leadership and conditions that better enable success. Other conditions include best practices in board governance in relation to recruitment and retention together with high standards of oversight and assessment; effective, efficient governance;

and a policy environment that facilitates planning. Preparation is important too, though in short supply in view of weak succession planning for the university's highest office. Reconsideration of what is in effect a presumption in favour of external candidates would be a first step in improving succession planning; only then would mentorship in preparing for the office be possible.

Dismissals and pressured early departures from presidential offices continue. They may occur for one or more of three reasons: corruption, though this is rare; major errors on important files; and embarrassing the university in the eyes of its alumni, supporters, and the general public. Some presidential contracts provide for dismissal without cause, thereby exposing presidents to dismissal on account of changes in board leadership or membership, abrupt shifts in expectations of their offices, and unpopularity for reasons good or bad.

In May 2014 the University of Saskatchewan dismissed its president of less than two years. The decision to do so crystallized in the firing by the administration of the executive director of the university's school of public health, Robert Buckingham, from both his administrative post and tenured academic position. He took issue with the university administration's plans for his school, and with its expectations that he would support those plans – in public and with his own faculty and students – whether he agreed with them or not. His dismissal provoked a firestorm provincially, nationally, and beyond. The university's name was dragged through the mud. The provost resigned and the president was fired.

The case raised immediate issues relating to Buckingham's two offices. He enjoyed no tenure as an administrator, and if he was at odds with the university's stated plans for his school, he could step down as director, be invited to do so, or be discharged from his administrative position. But he could not be discharged as a professor for these reasons, and the administration's attempt to dismiss him from both offices ignited the firestorm.

More broadly, the case illustrates that freedom of speech must be considered along with academic freedom in matters of academic controversy. As a professor, Buckingham enjoyed the latter in teaching and research, and in matters bearing on his ability to engage in them without interference. That he could not claim academic freedom in his administrative duties did not leave him defenceless on differences with the president about them. University deans and directors of schools are in unique and difficult positions. They are formally accountable to presidents and provosts, and informally accountable to their faculty and students. They are not simply line managers obliged both to follow and publicly support orders. Moreover, in larger universities in which there are many deans, they constitute a vital council of the university and must be accorded wide latitude in articulating the views of their faculty and students, and in advancing and defending the professional standards of their disciplines. In short, they have freedom of speech as well as academic freedom.

Freedom of speech has limits, but in universities it must be accorded great respect if the merit of ideas is to hold sway over commands, pronouncements, and threats. Presidents must articulate and model this respect, and for this reason, they must have both patience and good communication skills. Their moral authority to lead is more important than their line authority to command, and to effect most of their plans they must rely on persuading their internal and external communities of their merits. Once the university's governing bodies – their senates and boards – have determined matters, the debate for administrators on their merits is over, but until that time it must be tolerated and encouraged. That time had not arrived at the University of Saskatchewan when Buckingham was discharged.

One of the criticisms of senates (council, in the terminology at University of Saskatchewan) is that they are dominated by administrators who have set agendas and voting commitments. The criticism has force if deans are instructed to line up dutifully behind the senior administration and to express no difference or dissent on matters affecting their faculties, programs, and students. The idea of debate is compromised when there are predetermined voting blocks of whatever composition in deliberative bodies.

Robert Buckingham publicly criticized the administration for its plans for his school and for its efforts to ensure his public compliance with those plans. The administration overreacted in dismissing him from both his administrative and academic posts. The ensuing controversy over both academic freedom and freedom of speech was understandable and predictable in extent and severity, and it embarrassed the university at home and abroad. The university backtracked on Buckingham's dismissal from his academic post and restored his professorship in public health. The president paid for the imbroglio with her job.

Afterword: On the Global Talent Race

At dinner in Beijing I was seated beside the president of a prominent Chinese university. He described his country's plans to build one hundred of the best universities in the world in the twenty-first century. It was not the first I had heard of this ambition. I had noted on an extended trip to China that it was voiced by university, government, and public and private sector leaders alike, and that they appeared to be determined as well as united behind the goal. "Where will you get the faculty?," I asked my host. He replied that many of the faculty would come from China's best universities. "The rest," he said, "we will get from you."

By this he meant that to secure the necessary talent to build its university system, China would compete globally for faculty, including recruitment of expatriate Chinese and other faculty from western universities. Whether the country would do so successfully was not the point; it was the clear goal and its cross-sectoral and determined pursuit that were striking. Of course there are differences between Canada and China that make this ambition more pressing in the latter. Its fast-tracked development highlighted its talent deficit and made remediation an urgent priority, and the country's internal conditions meant that concerted pursuit of that goal would follow. But it is the goal itself that should be emphasized: it is talent; it can be identified anywhere in the world and it can move to anywhere in the world.

There should be no doubt about the extent and rapidity of change in the environment in which our universities find themselves. In *The Great Brain Race*[1] Ben Wildavsky records "the growing globalization of higher education in all its dimensions: the evermore intense recruitment of students and faculty; the swift spread of branch campuses;

the well-financed efforts to create world-class universities, whether by upgrading existing institutions or by building brand new ones; the innovative efforts by online universities and other for-profit players to fill unmet needs in higher education markets around the globe; and the closely watched rankings by which everyone keeps score."[2] The implications for Canada are clear. We are in the great brain race, whether we like it or not; there is an unpersuasive counter-narrative that associates globalization with the corporate university and wishes it would go away. It will not.

Identifying the right policy answers requires that we ask the right policy questions, and these, at least, are clear. Where does Canada wish to locate itself in the world described by Wildavsky? Does it even make sense to speak of "Canadian" wishes on this subject, or is it possible to speak only of the accumulation of the disparate policies of ten provinces, three territories, and the federal government? What are the respective goals of federal, provincial, and municipal governments in advancing higher education policy? What are the roles of universities, both in ensuring that the right questions are asked and in preparing themselves to help answer those questions?

There is ambiguity in public policy affecting Canadian universities, which has origins partly in complacency. We are a fortunate people in a fortunate country; we have some excellent universities and several very good ones. We begin the talent race with advantages, but how we place will depend on building on our advantages, not resting on them. Another source of ambiguity is our federal state with divided jurisdiction in post-secondary education and research – a division that makes it difficult to contemplate and articulate common goals, let alone pursue them. And we should not overlook culture as a potential source of ambiguity. Declarations of lofty goals are not typical of Canadians, and our great efforts in nation-building tend to be recognized in hindsight rather than announced in advance.

This ambiguity may persist. Newton's first law of motion predicates constant velocity unless interrupted by force, a law of physics that again brings to mind path dependency: established ways are ways of least resistance because they are positively reinforced by influences accustomed to those established ways. They can be disrupted by crisis though not easily by threats, and the threat of a talent loss is neither so imminent nor so graphic as to produce urgent will and energy to avert it. This is where leadership really matters. Leaders can disrupt an established path if they recognize the importance of doing so and the need to chart an alternative course. Establishing Canada as a talent magnet is a revised course worthy of pursuit.

There should at least be common ground on our goals in the global competition for talent: we should strive to retain top Canadian students and graduates and to attract the best international students and faculty to our universities. We should be, and be known widely to be, their preferred choice. This will require better national and local public policy, and in this respect the government's announcement in January 2014 that it would implement the Chakma Report is welcome.[3] It will also require our universities to up their game. Each must position itself with regard not only to its history, public expectations, and current standing, but to the new world described by Wildavsky. Done well, this would advance a more explicit differentiation among our universities, and this is desirable in a context in which greater clarity is needed around their different missions, goals, and plans. This process should include acknowledgment by universities, their communities, and governments that Canada would benefit by having more universities included among the best in the world. They cannot be preordained in name and number; competition must determine which ones and how many, and the competition should be welcomed and supported.

Universities do not properly position themselves by proclaiming high ambitions and touting them in the absence of a framework that includes their histories, capacities, and limitations; they do so through strategic planning based – in Giamatti's words – on a "practical and compelling" vision, one that is developed collegially and with supportive communities. Those supportive communities include governments and they, too, must up their games. In important respects the federal government has done this over the past two decades, though huge gaps remain in research policy and support, particularly in the sciences. Provincial governments' attention to their universities is more accurately described as behaviour than as policy. Preoccupied by more immediate and pressing concerns, including health care, most of them pay little attention to the global competition for talent, and to the variable capacities of their universities to participate and place well in that competition. And the attention they do give their universities is often uneven, parochial, and ill informed. There is no better example than the cumulative record of our provinces on the matter of tuition. Instead of being seen as one dimension of a comprehensive package on access, quality, and capacity, tuition is treated as a pawn in elaborate public relations rituals involving governments with their publics, the universities, and particularly the students.

The global talent race engages civic governments and organizations in addition to federal and provincial ones. Talent is one of Richard Florida's "three T's" of successful cities; the other two are technology and tolerance.[4] Universities and the cities in which they are located have a mutual interest in one another's success, and a strong partnership is the best expression of this interest. University and civic leaders should know one another and mutually support their efforts to attract talent that will enhance university and city life and prospects.

The competition for talent will demand other changes of our universities. Administrations and boards of governors must recover and re-establish board authority to set tuition. They are in the best position to determine what rates are necessary for their institutions to do their work well. Theirs is the governance responsibility for university finances, and many provincial governments have usurped that authority, sometimes contrary to their own legislation. In so doing they have deprived boards of important leverage in discharging their fiduciary responsibility. It is not open to governments to claim that they had to act in the face of irresponsible tuition increases. In pricing their courses and programs, universities are subject to market discipline, and their internal politics make boards very sensitive in the matter; their record in containing tuition increases was a good one. Governments became involved because of the perceived political sensitivity of the issue, but instead of leaving responsibility where it belonged – in the hands of boards many of whose members they appointed – they made it even more politically sensitive by regulating it. This should end. There is ample room for governments to influence universities in their setting of tuition without intervening to freeze, unfreeze, regulate, mandate, or otherwise direct them in the matter. Provincial governments have the responsibility of deciding how much of their revenues they will commit to support universities for which they garner credit or criticism, as with other expenditures. They should leave to universities the task of determining the implications of this for tuition rates.

I have argued in chapter 3 for a more systematic approach to cost based on an equal apportionment of public/private benefits of a post-secondary education. Provincial governments would commit to paying 50 per cent of the full costs to the universities of mounting their programs, while participating with the federal government in offering loans to students to cover the other 50 per cent, together with a stipend to cover living costs, which are typically higher than tuition. These loans would be repayable on an income-contingent basis. Whether using this or any other approach, tuition should reflect a reasoned, transparent position on where costs should lie and how they can be paid, so as to ensure that all students qualified to undertake a university education have the opportunity to do so.

Universities must also become better at partnership. It is not a philanthropic arrangement; it is a relationship developed through shared interests. Universities are not ivory towers, and they have many existing and potential interests to share with public and private sector organizations of all kinds. If their expertise is not made available through partnership, reliance will increase on consultancies, and the former offer greater potential benefits and opportunities for universities than the latter. They are properly vigilant to protect both their core missions and academic freedom, and their partners usually understand their need to do so; indeed the integrity of research protected by academic freedom is in the interests of all concerned. In chapter 5 I described three examples that yield additional guidance in the development of these partnerships: address governance early, relying on expert advice where necessary; where the partnership results in a new entity, ensure that its leadership has the authority necessary to give it an identity distinct from any or all of the partners; make donor agreements public; and be clear about the distinction between giving advice and decision-making authority.

Strengthening bicameral governance and protecting it from unwarranted intrusion will be vital to the future success of Canadian universities. Reference is made above to interference by provincial governments in what should be boards of governors' decisions to set tuition rates. An equal threat is the encroachment of faculty unions upon the domain of boards and senates. Faculty unions are mandated to protect and advance the employment interests of their members; they are not mandated to co-manage universities or to displace and diminish the authority of their governing bodies. The legal and cultural norms of trade unionism, imported from industrial organization into the public sector, including most Canadian universities, are not compatible with a broader role in their management or governance. Moreover, faculty union and CAUT initiatives to diminish senates (usually statutory bodies entrusted by legislatures with plenary academic authority) invite intervention from governments if university administrations are unsuccessful in resisting them.

The governance of universities is both unique and delicate; it involves a dispersal of what in other organizations would be board and managerial authority to include a body of faculty, administration, and students to oversee and approve the universities' academic affairs. This broader dispersal of authority in universities to include faculty in academic governance and collegial management is essential to their success. But it involves risks when faculty are also members of trade unions. One risk is conflict of interest, and it is not adequately met by the common insistence that faculty simply change hats when they move from union business to collegial matters. Indeed this claim clearly fails in the context of a power struggle between senates and faculty unions. Conflict is clear in this situation. One implication is that faculty members holding executive or appointed office in their union should not concurrently be members of senates.

Because their governance is unique and delicate, it requires constant stewardship within universities. Presidents bear primary responsibility for ensuring good governance, though they share the burden with others, including board and senate chairs and members. In the case of public universities, it also requires vigilance by government to ensure that the unique governance of universities is not compromised by failures in this stewardship or encroachment through collective bargaining on the powers of boards, senates, and their responsible officers. In chapter 4, I conclude that a statutory framework may be needed to ensure that the terms and conditions of employment that are the focus of collective bargaining do not include governance arrangements that are the responsibility of legislatures and those entrusted by them with university leadership.

Boards of governors have become more conscious, insistent, and active in turning their attention to the requirements of good board governance. Senates need to do the same in their sphere of academic responsibility, and they are willing to do so. The study by Pennock et al. of Canadian university senates reveals that senates are aware of greater attention focused on governance and are attentive to areas needing improvement: their size and effectiveness, their linkages to boards and administrations, the importance of engaging more faculty in their work, a greater role in monitoring academic quality, and the need for self-assessment. University administrations should encourage and support efforts by senates to strengthen their roles in university governance, while resisting efforts by faculty unions to encroach upon their statutory jurisdiction through collective bargaining.

Universities must also bring greater clarity to the meaning of academic freedom. It should be a core value – not only of universities – but of society generally. But there remain strong differences within the academy about its reach, and confusion beyond about its meaning; how can universities expect broad public support for a concept of such ambiguity? I have argued that academic freedom is to be understood in relation to teaching and research, and the independence of faculty work in these activities. I have argued, too, that it must be distinguished from freedom of speech and that the extent of its protection must be assessed against a backdrop of contract, employment law, and human rights protection that did not exist when tenure was conceived. Universities, individually and collectively, must place themselves in a better position to assure their communities and supporters that academic freedom exists to protect the integrity of teaching and research, and that its invocation and availability are for these purposes, and these purposes only.

Leadership is another area requiring attention. The demands of university leaders have changed without commensurate changes in authority, and in the selection, preparation, and support of presidents. The dismissals or premature departures, in recent years, of significant numbers of Canadian university presidents is a warning signal; the fact that some of the most highly respected present and former university presidents in the country are ambivalent about whether presidents can make a difference, or are uncertain about what difference they can make, is another one.[5] I argue that presidents and their teams should have more authority in identifying leaders from department heads to vice-presidents, and that they should retain or recover a substantive role in tenure decisions. It merits repeating that these decisions represent multi-million-dollar investments. The role of boards in making these investments is a substantive one, which means that the role of the boards' senior advisors must be substantive as well.

A rethinking of presidential recruitment and selection processes is also desirable. Presidents must have qualifications and backgrounds that command respect in the academy. They need not have lived their lives in universities or come exclusively from its academic ranks. Senior administrative talent comes in many forms and guises, and the issue for boards in appointing presidents is aligning university needs with particular strengths of candidates. In doing so they should not be contained by outdated orthodoxies that strongly favour academic administrators over others, and external candidates over internal ones. The latter disposition has the added disadvantage of precluding or compromising succession planning for presidential offices.

The global talent race issues a challenge to universities, governments, and their broader communities to have a more informed and mature conversation about their mutual expectations and goals. At the centre of this conversation will be quality and service. Improving quality must become important to all our universities, more urgently to some than others, and the best international standards must be the guides if our country is to succeed in the talent race. Service to their students, in programs and resources, and to other organizations, including governments, in the form of partnerships, must be part of quality improvement. Determination combined with results-based governance and management will be required for success. It must be emphasized that determination on the part of universities will not be sufficient. Governments and broader communities must share an informed determination to see our universities be the best they can be, and they must hold themselves, as well as their universities, to account for the results. In short, we all need to get our act together.

Notes

1. Guess Who's Coming to Breakfast: On Positioning and Differentiation

1 The *Maclean's* University Rankings, Toronto.
2 For example, in 2006, eleven Canadian universities boycotted the rankings.
3 A group of fifteen research-intensive universities: Dalhousie, Laval, McGill, McMaster, Queen's, and the universities of Alberta, British Columbia, Calgary, Manitoba, Montréal, Ottawa, Saskatchewan, Toronto, Waterloo, and Western Ontario.
4 Nineteen universities attended the inaugural meeting of the Alliance of Canadian Comprehensive Research Universities (ACCRU) in 2011.
5 The universities were Alberta, British Columbia, McGill, Montreal, and Toronto. "Our Universities Can Be Smarter," *Maclean's*, 28 July 2009.
6 The Academic Ranking of World Universities (ARWU) is undertaken by researchers at Shanghai Jiao Tong University and published by Shanghai Ranking Consultancy.
7 Begun in 2007, the ranking is done by the Higher Education Evaluation and Accreditation Council of Taiwan and is based on eight indicators representing the criteria of research productivity, research improvement, and research excellence.
8 The QS World University Rankings are based on data covering research, employability, teaching, and internationalization, and are published in the United Kingdom by Quacquarelli Symonds Limited. The World University Rankings assess teaching, research, knowledge transfer, and international outlook and are published by Thomson Reuters.
9 Mark Kingwell, "A University Education Is More Valuable Than Any 'Outcome,'" *Globe and Mail*, 31 August 2013, http://www.theglobeandmail.com/.

10 Ibid.

11 Ibid.

12 Allan Tupper, "Pushing Federalism to the Limit: Post Secondary Education Policy in the Milennium," 2009, http://www.politics.ubc.ca/fileadmin/user_upload/poli_sci/Graduate/Cdn_Com/Tupper_Pushing_Federalism_to_the_Limit.pdf, 10.

13 In part because of the historically low levels of business investment or research and development in Canada. In 2008, Canada ranked eighteenth among countries measured in business expenditure on research and development, as a percentage of GDP (Science, Technology and Innovation Council, *State of the Nation 2010: Canada's Science, Technology and Innovation System*, http://www.stic-csti.ca/eic/site/stic-csti.nsf/eng/h_00038.html). Universities conduct 38 per cent of Canadian research, the highest percentage among G7 countries. AUCC, "Universities: Putting Ideas to Work for Canadians," pre-budget submission to the minister of finance, 2012, 2.

14 Competition Review Panel, *Compete to Win: Final Report* (June 2008).

15 Conference Board of Canada, *How Canada Performs: A Report Card on Canada* (2007).

16 Council of Canadian Academies, *Innovation and Business Strategy: Why Canada Falls Short* (2009).

17 Science, Technology and Innovation Council of Canada, *Imagination and Innovation: Building Canadian Paths to Prosperity* (2011).

18 Innovation Canada, *A Call to Action: Review of Federal Support to Research and Development – Expert Panel Report* (2011), http://rd-review.ca/eic/site/033.nsf/vwapj/R-D_InnovationCanada_Final-eng.pdf/$FILE/R-D_InnovationCanada_Final-eng.pdf.

19 Council of Canadian Academics, *The State of Science and Technology in Canada* (2011).

20 Also see chapter 4.

21 Academica Top Ten, 3 December 2013.

22 University of Saskatchewan Archives, Murray Papers, Walter Murray to Walter Scott. Murray was reminiscing about Scott's words to him years before.

23 Quoted in Michael Hayden, *Seeking a Balance: University of Saskatchewan, 1907–1982* (Vancouver: UBC Press, 1983), 26.

24 For example, George Britnell, R. MacGregor Dawson, Gerhard Herzberg, Harold Johns, C.J. Mackenzie, Hilda Neatby, Donald Rawson, W.P. Thompson, Thorbergur Thorvaldson, Mabel Timlin, Frank Underhill, and Norman Ward.

25 *President's Report 1908–9*, 12.

26 *President's Report 1912–13, 1913–14*, 1.
27 By, among others, the author of the first commissioned history of the university. See Hayden, *Seeking a Balance*.
28 Ibid.
29 Its roots go back to 1911 when Regina College was established by the Methodist Church. It was a junior college affiliated with the University of Saskatchewan from 1934 to 1959 when it achieved degree-granting status as the Regina campus of the U of S.
30 There was a historical tension between Regina and Saskatoon dating back to the decision to locate the university in Saskatoon in 1908. It was likely, if not inevitable, that the tension would play out to the establishment of a second university.
31 *Saskatchewan Universities Commission Survey of University Fiscal Systems* (1976).
32 Minutes of the ninth meeting of the Saskatchewan Universities Commission Funding Review Committee, 20 June 1978, University of Saskatchewan Archives.
33 Memo, Leo Kristjanson and R.G. Klombies to Board of Governors of the University of Saskatchewan, 28 March 1983.
34 This was the stated purpose of the appointment.
35 *Report of the Minister's Special Representative on University Revitalization, Mr Harold MacKay*, Q.C. (1996).
36 *Saskatchewan Universities Funding Review Final Report* (1998).
37 MacKinnon diary, 1:40, author's collection.
38 Ibid., 1:44.
39 The record of this meeting was made by the author in a memorandum immediately following the meeting, author's collection.
40 MacKinnon diary, 5:50.
41 In my first eight years as president of the University of Saskatchewan, I worked with eight ministers responsible for post-secondary education – an average of one a year.
42 Kevin Lynch, "Is Science and Technology up to the Task of Shaping Canada @150?," Killam Lecture 2012, 3.
43 Ibid.
44 Richard Florida, for example.
45 Richard Florida, *Cities and the Creative Class* (New York: Routledge, 2005).
46 MacKinnon diary, 1:12.
47 Ibid.
48 At the laying of the cornerstone for the university's College Building, 29 July 1910, Canada's seventh prime minister, Sir Wilfrid Laurier,

remarked, "There is no doubt that this university will in time be one of the world's greatest." University of Saskatchewan Archives, Miscellaneous Collection, 2069.2.

49 Late in the interview stage I was asked about my plans for housing. I indicated what was then my preference to remain in my own home. The cold reaction of the search committee led me to recant and to assure them that I would live in the university's on-campus president's residence.

50 *International Education: A Key Driver of Canada's Future Prosperity*, Report of the Advisory Panel on Canada's International Strategy (2012).

51 China, India, Brazil, the Middle East, and North Africa, in addition to traditional markets in the United States, France, and the United Kingdom.

52 Academica Top Ten, 16 January 2014.

53 Don Tapscott and Anthony Williams write, "The transformation of the university is not just a good idea – it is an imperative" and call for fundamental change in how learning is achieved (collaborative learning) and in the content of higher education. "If universities open up and embrace collaborative learning and collaborative knowledge production, they have a chance of surviving and even thriving in the networked, global economy." Tapscott and Williams, *Macrowikinomics* (Toronto: Penguin, 2012), 141.

54 The ten universities were Alberta, British Columbia, Laval, McGill, McMaster, Montréal, Queen's, Toronto, Waterloo, and Western Ontario.

55 U15 data, Ottawa, 2012.

56 RE$EARCH Infosource, 2 November 2012, www.researchinfosource.com.

57 Canadian Light Source; Vaccine and Infectious Disease Organization, International Vaccine Centre.

2. What's the Plan?: On the Pursuit of Goals

1 The expression may be a misquotation of Mao Zedong who urged that a "hundred flowers blossom."

2 For example, universities were required to submit research plans in order to participate in post-1995 competitive research funding.

3 Henry Mintzberg, *The Rise and Fall of Strategic Planning* (New York: Free Press, 1994), 18–23.

4 Ibid.

5 Ibid., 12.

6 Ann Korschgen, Rex Fuller, and Leo Lambert, "Institutional Planning That Makes a Difference," *AAHE Bulletin* 52, no. 8 (April 2000).

7 Ibid., 1.

8 Ibid., 2.

9 Ibid., 4.

10 Ibid., 4.

11 Michael Hayden, "The History of Planning at the University of Saskatchewan," *University of Saskatchewan Faculty Association Bulletin*, 6 December 2002.

12 The initiative was announced but was stillborn, P. MacKinnon diary, 3:54.

13 Tim Quigley, "The Integrated Planning Process Violates the University of Saskatchewan Act, 1995," *University of Saskatchewan Faculty Association Bulletin*, 6 January 2003.

14 Two members of the government caucus reported the views of several of their colleagues. P. MacKinnon diary 5:5.

15 George Keller, *Academic Strategy: The Management Revolution in American Higher Education* (Baltimore: Johns Hopkins University Press, 1983), viii.

16 Ibid., 115.

17 Ibid., 140.

18 Ibid., 140–51.

19 The Faculty Association argued that because the collective agreement referred to Council, the body could not be restructured and reformed without the association's consent.

20 VP (Special Projects) – BA Holmlund, RG 2006-2, series 9: Issues and Options, file 42, Governance – Final Report, 1989, University of Saskatchewan Archives.

21 University of Saskatchewan Act (1995).

22 "A Framework for Planning at the University of Saskatchewan" (1998).

23 Interview with Michael Atkinson, 13 January 2013.

24 "The Provost's White Paper on Integrated Planning" (2002), 4.

25 Ibid., 6.

26 Interview with Michael Atkinson, 13 January 2013.

27 Ibid.

28 "A Framework for Action: University of Saskatchewan Integrated Plan 2003–2007."

29 "Toward an Engaged University: University of Saskatchewan Integrated Plan 2008–2012."

30 "Promise and Potential: University of Saskatchewan Integrated Plan 2012–2016."

31 Provost Atkinson, "The Academic Agenda: Progress and Prospects," 3 March 1999.

32 "The Academic Agenda: A 'Report Card' on Integrated Planning," 27 February 2006.

33 Provost Atkinson, "2011 Academic Address," 3.
34 Ibid., 4.
35 According to Laura Kennedy, head of the university's Financial Services
    Division, the operating budget in 2000/1 was $200.3 million and in
    2012/13 was $453 million, an increase of 226 per cent. Email to author,
    16 September 2013.
36 The Canadian Light Source, a third-generation synchrotron, and the
    International Vaccine Centre, a facility capable of containment for
    infectious disease and vaccines research with large animals.
37 See, for example, Paul Pierson, "Increasing Returns, Path Dependence
    and the Study of Politics," *American Political Science Revue* 94, no. 2 (2000):
    251–67; and Paul A. David, "Path Dependence: A Foundational Concept
    for Historical Social Science," *Cliometrica: The Journal of Historical Economics
    and Econometric History* 1, no. 2 (2007): 91–114.
38 David, "Path Dependence," 1.

3. White Coats Make an Office Call: On Tuition
and Financial Assistance for Students

 1 In Ontario the Wright Commission (1972) proposed raising tuition to a
    level representing one-third to one-half of instructional costs. In Alberta
    the Worth Commission (1972) recommended that fees be raised to 25 per
    cent of program costs in order to reduce lower-income-group subsidies of
    higher education for students from higher income groups. In Manitoba the
    Oliver Task Force (1973) proposed no change in the 18 per cent of program
    costs represented by tuition. In Nova Scotia the Graham Commission
    (1974) suggested that students should pay the full instructional costs of
    their university education. These were followed in the 1980s by further
    studies in Ontario and Nova Scotia. Since then there have been additional
    studies including Bob Rae, *Ontario: A Leader in Learning* (2005), known also
    as the Rae Report; and K. Norrie and M.C. Lennon, *Tuition Fee Policy Options
    for Ontario* (Toronto: Higher Education Quality Council of Ontario, 2011).
 2 David Stager, *Focus on Fees: Alternative Policies for University Tuition Fees*
    (Toronto: Council of Ontario Universities, 1989).
 3 Ibid., 18, 19.
 4 Ibid., 45.
 5 Ibid., 46, 47.
 6 Ibid., 63.
 7 Ibid., 64.
 8 Ibid.

9 Newfoundland and Labrador may feature practices that come as close as any to what can be described as policy in this area. The province has continuing challenges in sustaining and growing population numbers, which since 1999 have encouraged stay-at-home incentives of low tuition. Before then, tuition fees in the province were close to the Canadian average. Since then they have been reduced, so that they are presently at about 50 per cent of the Canadian average.

10 In my thirteen years as president of the University of Saskatchewan I was involved in many discussions of tuition levels. In earlier years they were one-off conversations, reactive to circumstances peculiar to a particular budget and never inviting debate about underlying policy and evidence supporting different views on the subject. On one occasion I was asked by a Cabinet minister facing imminent budget finalization how much the cost of tuition would be reduced by a 0.5 per cent increase in the operating budget. In the later years of the NDP government of Lorne Calvert and the early years of the Saskatchewan Party government of Brad Wall, conversation with ministry officials was more deliberate, policy oriented, and timely. The result was annual letters recording understandings about tuition levels that might be set by the university in anticipation of government grants at a particular level. This approach worked well and took into account the political sensitivity of tuition issues while deferring to the legislated authority of the university to establish its own tuitions.

11 Rae Report, 23.

12 Ibid., 13.

13 Ibid., 23, 24.

14 Norrie and Lennon, *Tuition Fee Policy Options*. See note 1.

15 Ibid., 5.

16 Ibid.

17 Ibid., 9.

18 Ibid., 9.

19 Ibid., 11.

20 Alex Usher and Patrick Duncan, *Beyond the Sticker Shock: A Closer Look at Canadian Tuition Fees* (Toronto: Education Policy Institute, 2008).

21 Ibid.

22 Janice MacKinnon, *Health Care Reform from the Cradle of Medicare* (Ottawa: MacDonald-Laurier Institute, 2013), 15.

23 Ibid.

24 Rae Report, 18.

25 Ibid.

26 Ibid.

27 Warren McCall, *Post-Secondary Education Accessibility and Affordability Review: Final Report* (2007).

28 Newfoundland and Labrador, and Quebec vie for the lowest university tuition in Canada.

29 *Globe and Mail*, editorial, 23 March 2012.

30 David Coletto, "The National Implications of the Student Protests in Quebec," *iPOLITICS*, 23 May 2012.

31 Bill 78, An Act to Enable Students to Receive Instruction from the Postsecondary Institutions They Attend.

32 Heather Munroe-Blum, "PQ's Decision to Cancel Tuition Leaves Universities in the Red," *Montreal Gazette*, 5 September 2012.

33 "On Campus," *Macleans.ca*, 20 September 2012.

34 Pierre Fortin, presentation to a round table at L'Institut du Nouveau-Monde, Laval University, 26 January 2013.

35 Ibid.

36 W. Craig Riddell, "The Social Benefits of Education: New Evidence on an Old Question," in *Taking Public Universities Seriously*, ed. Frank Iacobucci and Carolyn Tuohy, 138–63 (Toronto: University of Toronto Press, 2005). Dr Riddell writes that although more research is needed, particularly more Canadian research, "the value of the social benefits of education appears to be similar in size to the private market returns to education from higher lifetime earnings" (159).

37 Rae Report, 22.

38 Ibid.

39 Ibid.

40 Norrie and Lennon, *Tuition Fee Policy Options*, 16.

4. Yes Minister: On Government Engagement, Academic Freedom, and Collective Advocacy

1 Paul Davidson, "University Is Still the Surest Path to Prosperity," *Globe and Mail*, 3 September 2012.

2 Ibid.

3 Ben Levin, *Governing Education* (Toronto: University of Toronto Press, 2005).

4 Ibid., 13.

5 In conversation with the author.

6 Levin, *Governing Education*, 23.

7 Ibid., 69.

8 Ibid.

9 Ibid.

10 Ibid.

11 Ian Clark, Greg Moran, Michael Skolnik, and David Trick, *Academic Transformation: The Forces Reshaping Higher Education in Ontario* (Montreal and Kingston: McGill-Queen's University Press, 2009).

12 Ibid., 138–42.

13 Ibid., 150.

14 Ibid.

15 Ibid., 145.

16 Ibid., 169, 170.

17 Ibid., 170.

18 Ibid., 169.

19 An acronym for *Collège d'enseignement général et professionnel*, known officially in English as a "general and vocational college." It refers to the public post-secondary education collegiate institutions exclusive to the education system in the province of Quebec in Canada.

20 Clark et al., *Academic Transformation*, 169.

21 Ibid., 138.

22 Ibid., 178.

23 Ibid., 185.

24 George Fallis, *Multiversities, Ideas and Democracy* (Toronto: University of Toronto Press, 2007).

25 Ibid., 381. The word *multiversity* typically refers to a university with many constituent parts: faculties, schools, research institutes, sometimes on more than one campus. It might refer to a university system rather than a single institution.

26 Ibid., 384.

27 Ibid.

28 Ibid.

29 Ibid., 381, 382.

30 Peter MacKinnon, "Administering and Protecting Academic Freedom," in *Pursuing Academic Freedom: Free and Fearless?*, ed. Len Findlay and Paul Bidwell (Saskatoon: Purich Publishing, 2001), 38. The influence of this definition can be seen in AUCC, "Canada's Universities Adopt a New Statement on Academic Freedom," news release, 25 October 2011, http://www.aucc.ca/media-room/news-and-commentary/canadas-universities-adopt-new-statement-on-academic-freedom/.

31 Ibid.

32 Fallis, *Multiversities*, 340.

33 Ibid., 341.

34 Ibid.

35 Ibid., 343.
36 Ibid., 344.
37 Ibid., 346.
38 Ibid., 347.
39 Ibid.
40 Ibid., 350.
41 Ibid., 351.
42 Ibid., 352.
43 Ibid., 347.
44 Ibid., 359–61.
45 AUCC, www.aucc.ca.
46 Interview with Martha Piper, 10 January 2014.
47 Ibid.
48 See also chapter 5.

5. Grateful Dogs: On Philanthropy, Commercialization, and Partnerships

1 Imagine Canada is a national organization established in 2005 to advance the cause of charitable and non-profit organizations. It was formed by the union of the Canadian Centre of Philanthropy and the Coalition of National Voluntary Organizations.
2 Derek Bok, *Universities in the Marketplace: The Commercialization of Higher Education* (Princeton: Princeton University Press, 2003), 6.
3 Examples from my experience include saying no to an offer of a $500,000 endowment to support scholarships upon a condition that barred Aboriginal students as recipients because the donor felt they had adequate financial support from government; and declining a million dollar donation in support of food safety research where the prospective donor pressed his expectations about research outcomes.
4 Bok, *Universities in the Marketplace*, 3.
5 Ibid., 1.
6 Ibid., 5.
7 Ibid., 10.
8 Ibid., 11.
9 Ibid.
10 This legislation, writes Bok, "made it much easier for universities to own and licence patents on discoveries made through research paid for with public funds." Ibid., 11.
11 Ibid., 13, 14.

12 Ibid., 14.

13 Ibid., 24, 25.

14 Ibid., 30.

15 Ibid., 32.

16 Ibid., 54.

17 Ibid., 55.

18 Ibid., 56.

19 Ibid., 77.

20 Academica Top Ten, 13 June 2013. See also note 29.

21 Bok, *Universities in the Marketplace*, 98.

22 Ibid., 104.

23 Ibid.

24 Ibid., 108.

25 Ibid., 118.

26 Ibid., 121.

27 Ibid.

28 Jennifer Washburn, *University Inc.: The Corporate Corruption of Higher Education* (New York: Basic Books, 2005).

29 Ibid., 228.

30 Ibid.

31 "U of Toronto Lectures Coloured by Big Pharma: Study," *Toronto Star*, 12 June 2013.

32 As reported in "Highlights of OECD-FAO Agricultural Outlook, 2012–2021," *Globe and Mail*, 5 June 2013, A8.

33 Ibid.

34 Innovation Place. See also chapter 7.

35 Interview with Wayne Brownlee, 22 May 2013.

36 Ibid.

37 Ibid.

38 Interview with Alanna Koch, 24 May 2013.

39 Ibid.

40 Ibid.

41 Department website, http://carleton.ca/political management.

42 Clayton H. Riddell Graduate Program in Political Management Donor Agreement, 4 May 2010.

43 Ibid., Appendix A.

44 Ibid.

45 Editorial, *Globe and Mail*, 13 July 2012.

46 Letter to Carleton community, 24 July 2012.

47 Balsillie School of International Affairs, "BSIA Governance Document (Final)."

48 Interview with Thomas Homer-Dixon, 3 June 2013.
49 CAUT, "Investigation into the Termination of Dr Ramesh Thakur as
    Director of the Balsillie School of International Affairs, Affiliated with the
    University of Waterloo, Wilfrid Laurier University, and the Waterloo-based
    Centre for International Governance Innovation" (2010).
50 Interview with Thomas Homer-Dixon.
51 Interview with Rohinton Medhora, 3 June 2013.
52 Balsillie School of International Affairs, "BSIA Governance Document
    (Final)," 1.
53 Ibid.
54 John Ravinhill, whose appointment was announced on 3 June 2013.
55 Balsillie School of International Affairs, "BSIA Governance Document
    (Final)," Annex C.
56 Ibid., Annex G.
57 Ibid.
58 Ibid., Annex E.
59 Homer-Dixon, http://www.homerdixon.com/wp-content/uploads/
    2012/04/Response-to-CAUT-private-think-tank-claim.pdf.
60 *Toronto Star*, 27 April 2012.
61 CAUT, "Guiding Principles for University Collaborations" (2012).
62 Ibid.
63 Ibid., 6.
64 Ibid., 7.
65 Ibid.
66 Ibid., 6.
67 Thomas Homer-Dixon, "What are CAUT's *real* motives?," http://
    www.homerdixon.com/wp-content/uploads/2012/04/CAUTs-motives6
    .pdf.
68 "Academic integrity depends on independence – The case of Balsillie,"
    University World News, 10 June 2012.
69 Ibid.
70 Memorandum of Understanding among the Centre for International
    Governance and Innovation, University of Waterloo, and Wilfrid Laurier
    University, October 2012.
71 Ibid.
72 Lindsay Purchase, "Local universities free from censure," *The Cord*,
    28 November 2012, www.thecord.ca.
73 Chapter 4.

6. Let's Make a Deal: On Governance, Collegial Management, and Collective Bargaining

1 Lea Pennock, Glen A. Jones, Jeff M. Leclerc, and Sharon X. Li, "Academic Senates and University Governance: Changes in Structure and Perceptions of Senate Members" (paper presented at the Annual Meeting of the Consortium of Higher Education Researchers, Belgrade, Serbia, 2012).

2 Ibid.

3 Eleven at the University of Saskatchewan, more than sixty – at one time – at Bishop's University. While the optimum size of a board of governors is debatable, it is far closer to eleven than to sixty. In the author's view, the number should not exceed eighteen. At least two-thirds of the members should be neither employees of nor students at the university.

4 Pennock et al., "Academic Senates and University Governance."

5 Ibid.

6 Ibid.

7 Ibid.

8 Ibid.

9 Constitution of the Saskatchewan Federation of Labour, Article III, section 2.

10 In 2013 a new Labour-Management Relations Certificate program was launched, which featured joint training with union and management participants.

11 See www.mcgill.ca/maut.

12 The professoriate has never been self-governing in the sense that the legal and medical professions are. While it does have significant engagement in recruiting, hiring, and promoting university colleagues, it typically avoids discipline, a key responsibility of self-governance. The national organization (CAUT or the Canadian Association of University Teachers) is an advocacy organization, not a governance body.

13 J.R. Miller, *Vox* 1 (1987).

14 CAUT discussion paper (2004) quoted in *Report of the CAUT Ad Hoc Advisory Committee on Governance* (2009).

15 CAUT Policy Statement on Governance (2008).

16 *Report of the CAUT Ad Hoc Advisory Committee on Governance* (2009), 3.

17 Ibid.

18 *University of British Columbia v University of British Columbia and the Labour Relations Board,* B.C.C.A., 2007.

19 British Columbia University Act, R.S.B.C. 1996, c. 468, s. 59.

20 Administrative Tribunals Act, S.B.C. 2004, c. 45, SMS, s. 58.
21 *University of British Columbia v University of British Columbia Faculty Association* (B.C.S.C., 2006), 27.
22 *University of British Columbia Faculty Association v University of British Columbia and Labour Relations Board* (S.C.C., 2007).
23 *University of British Columbia v University of British Columbia and the Labour Relations Board,* B.C.C.A., 2007, 31.
24 Ibid.
25 The author was president at the time.
26 "In The Matter of an Arbitration Hearing and the Tenure of Dr Iliopoulou Pursuant to a Collective Bargaining Agreement between the University of Saskatchewan and the University of Saskatchewan Faculty Association" (2010).
27 Ibid., Administration Brief, 6.
28 Ibid., 7.
29 Pennock et al., "Academic Senates and University Governance."

7. A Canadian Dilemma: Strong Science, Weak Innovation

1 Michael Bancroft, "The Canadian Light Source History and Scientific Prospects," *Canadian Journal of Chemistry* 82, no. 6 (2004): 1028.
2 Ibid., 1030.
3 The team was established by President George Ivany, and its members included scientists Dennis Johnson and Dennis Skopik as well as university lawyer Douglas Richardson. Kent Campbell, Bernard Michel, John Wright, and Jim Yuel added private sector and government representation.
4 This was the initial capital cost only. Synchrotrons are developed in phases, as suites of beamlines are added. As of 2013, the total investment in the capital project is more than $350 million.
5 Chapter 1, 10.
6 Government of Canada (Science, Technology and Innovation Council), "Canada's Science, Technology and Innovation System: State of the Nation" (2008); and "Canada's Science, Technology and Innovation System: State of the Nation" (2010).
7 Council of Canadian Academies, Expert Panel on the State of Science and Technology in Canada. "The State of Science and Technology in Canada" (2012).
8 Government of Canada, "Canada's ... State of the Nation" (2008), 5.
9 Ibid., 5.
10 Ibid., 6.
11 Ibid.
12 Ibid.

13 Ibid., 23–5.
14 "Innovation Canada: A Call to Action," Report of the Independent Panel
    on Federal Support to Research and Development (2011). By their nature,
    cultural differences are imprecise and untraceable in any clear sense.
    Conversationally, it is often said that innovation is not strong in Canadian
    bloodstreams, with the result that it is not strong in Canadian business
    plans either.
15 Government of Canada, "Canada's ... State of the Nation" (2008), 7.
16 Ibid.
17 Ibid.
18 Ibid., 8.
19 Government of Canada, "Canada's ... State of the Nation" (2010).
20 Ibid., 1.
21 Ibid.
22 Ibid.
23 Ibid.
24 Ibid., 2.
25 Council of Canadian Academies, xii.
26 Ibid.
27 Ibid.
28 Ibid.
29 Ibid., 100.
30 Ibid., 111.
31 Ibid., 102.
32 Ibid., 102, 103.
33 Ibid., 116.
34 Conference Board of Canada, "A Report Card on Canada" (2007). In the
    2013 Report Card, Canada maintained its D ranking in innovation, www
    .conferenceboard.ca.
35 Ibid.
36 Industry Canada, *Compete to Win: Final Report* (2008), 18.
37 Janet Atkinson-Grosjean, *Public Science Private Interests: Culture and Commerce
    in Canada's Networks of Centres of Excellence* (Toronto: University of Toronto
    Press, 2006), 5.
38 Ibid., 19.
39 Ibid.
40 Ibid.
41 Ibid.
42 Ibid.
43 Ibid., 6.
44 Ibid.

45 Ibid., 7.
46 Ibid.
47 Ibid., 192.
48 Ibid., 192, 193.
49 Ibid., 193.
50 Ibid., 198.
51 Ibid., 199.
52 Ibid., 202.
53 "Innovation Canada: A Call to Action" Executive Summary.
54 Ibid.
55 Ibid.
56 Council of Canadian Academies, *The State of Industrial R&D in Canada*
    (Ottawa: Expert Panel on Industrial R&D in Canada, 2013). See also
    Council of Canadian Academies, *Paradox Lost: Exploring Canada's Research
    Strength and Innovation Weakness* (Ottawa: Advisory Group, Council of
    Canadian Academies, 2013).
57 Ibid., xi.
58 Ibid., xv.
59 Ibid., xvii.
60 Ibid.
61 Ibid.
62 The first and second CEOs of the CLS, both outstanding scientists.
63 Innovation Canada expert committee report: *Major Science Initiatives Fund*
    (2011), 4.
64 Association of Universities and Colleges of Canada, *Funding the
    Institutional Costs of Research: An International Perspective* (2009), 2.
65 Ibid., 16–18.
66 Tom Brzustowski, *Why We Need More Innovation in Canada and What We
    Must Do to Get It* (Ottawa: Invenire Books, 2012).
67 Ibid.
68 Ibid.
69 Ibid.
70 Ibid.
71 Ibid.
72 The ten principles are:

    1. Do no harm.
    2. Recognize that the cultures in the private and public sectors are very
       different, that innovation takes place differently, and that it must be
       supported, managed, and evaluated differently in the two sectors.

3. Support both the supply and demand sides of innovation in the private sector.
4. For innovation in the public sector, recalibrate the balance among innovation, speed, risk, and accountability, while involving the media.
5. Develop Canada's cultural diversity as an advantage in marketing Canadian value-added products in world markets.
6. Promote the export of value-added Canadian products and raw materials. Export Canadian innovations, not the Canadian capacity to innovate.
7. Encourage the development of a national capacity for modern value-added manufacturing so that Canadians might be able to make and sell what we invent.
8. Pay attention to new ventures that have found the financing to spend substantially more on R&D than they collect in sales revenues ... They need help with commercialization, not with R&D. They are very important because they are the only source of Canada's future large, innovative companies.
9. Provide incentives for patient long-term investment in successful new ventures, so that they might grow to a large enough scale to compete in world markets ...
10. Ensure that government programs of support for innovation are entirely consistent with the goals of the Innovation Action Plan and are organized and delivered as a system. Ibid., 319.

73 The nine program principles are:

1. Design program delivery to meet the needs of the demand side ...
2. Government doesn't pick winners; competition in the market does that ...
3. Mobilize government's purchasing power in support of innovation ...
4. Develop support programs through people with subject expertise and experience, and give them the authority to make spending decisions in the field, in a way that balances strict accountability with judgment.
5. The subject of IP rights is dynamic around the world. Don't get left behind because innovators will not stay where they will be disadvantaged.
6. Avoid a hardening of the categories ... Be ready to support an activity that is demonstrably needed to support innovation even if it is not yet included in any formal definition.
7. Recognize that research is not innovation, that generally in the private sector Innovation = Invention + Commercialization, and also that successful commercialization requires a business model that is appropriate to the invention.

8. Recognize that innovations have both technical and social dimensions and that in the private sector the balance of innovations will lean to the technical, and in the public sector innovations it will lean to the social.
9. Focus on quality. Support only excellent innovation, wherever it occurs. Ibid., 328–35.

74 Ibid., 177.
75 Ibid.
76 Ibid.
77 Chapter 5.
78 Brzustowski, 177.
79 Ibid.
80 Ibid., 185.
81 Ibid., 186, 187.
82 Atkinson-Grosjean, *Public Science Private Interests*, 202.
83 Porter's "main point was that it was companies that made a nation competitive, and that they were most competitive when they were part of a cluster of interacting companies that included all the services that they needed in their business, as well as competing companies in the sector." Ibid., 215.
84 Ibid., 218.
85 Some threats to Innovation Place were borne of parochialism. In its planning stages there were objections to locating a dining establishment and other recreational spaces on its campus, and local business interests periodically expressed concern about the park competing with them. Expansion at Innovation Place is viewed by some as coming at the expense of the downtown business community or other commercial districts in the city. Of course they overlook the fact that for core tenants of the park, the choice is to locate at Innovation Place or in another city. Successful innovation parks compete with one another, not with business districts in communities in which they are located. However, to this day, parochialism continues to impede and undermine the development of Innovation Place.

But the most serious threat to the park came in 2002. The province's Crown Investments Corporation moved to replace the park's excellent and experienced leadership team by a commercial real estate manager who had no experience with the important and specialized work of research parks. There had been no advance consultation with either the park's management advisory committee or the university. On Easter weekend, I invited the deputy minister to the premier and the president of the Crown Investments Corporation to join me and the management advisory

committee at my campus residence. A short time after this intense
meeting, the decision was reversed and the able leadership team remained
in place.

86 It was a unanimous choice by the judges who cited Innovation Place's
global reputation and positive impact on the cities of Saskatoon, Regina,
Prince Albert, the province's universities, and Saskatchewan as a whole.
Government of Saskatchewan, "International Award for Innovation
Place," news release, 23 October 2009.

87 Keith Downey is widely acclaimed as "The Father of Canola."

8. Leadership with an Asterisk: On the Precarious Presidency

1 Bart Giamatti was president of Yale University. I have seen this statement
attributed to him, though I have been unable to identify the precise source.
Sources contacted at Yale believe it may have been a commencement
address.

2 Ross H. Paul, *Leadership under Fire: The Challenging Role of the Canadian
University President* (Montreal and Kingston: McGill-Queen's University
Press, 2011).

3 Ibid., viii.

4 *Globe and Mail*, 3 August 2001.

5 *Globe and Mail*, 11 February 2009.

6 David H. Turpin, "Canadian University Presidents Project & Perceptions
of University Autonomy and Accountability," *Canadian Journal of Public
Administration* (forthcoming).

7 Paul, *Leadership under Fire*, viii.

8 Ibid., 226.

9 Ibid.

10 Ibid.

11 Ibid., 226, 227.

12 Ibid., 227.

13 Ibid., 228.

14 Ibid., 229.

15 Ibid., 229, 230.

16 Ibid., 230.

17 Ibid., 11.

18 Lea Pennock, Glen Jones, Jeff LeClerc, and Sharon Xiaoxu, "Issues and
Challenges for Collegial Self-Governance in Canada: Reflections on a
Survey of Academic Senates, 2013" (forthcoming).

19 Chapter 1.

20 Paul, *Leadership under Fire*, 32.

21 Ibid., 33, quoting an interview with Paul Davenport.

22 Stephen Trachtenberg, Gerald B. Kauvar, and E. Grady Bogue, *Presidencies Derailed: Why University Leaders Fail and How to Prevent It* (Baltimore: Johns Hopkins University Press, 2013).

23 Ibid.

24 Ibid., 7.

25 Ibid., 8.

26 *The Leadership Imperative: The Report of the AGB Task Force on the State of the Presidency in American Higher Education* (2006).

27 Association of Governing Boards, *Renewing the Academic Presidency: Stronger Leadership for Tougher Times* (1996) qtd in ibid., 8.

28 *The Leadership Imperative*, 8.

29 Ibid.

30 Ibid.

31 Ibid., 21.

32 Ibid.

33 Ibid., 23

34 Ibid., 28.

35 Paul, *Leadership under Fire*, 28.

36 Ibid., 27.

37 *The Leadership Imperative*, 21.

38 *National Post*, 18 July 2013, A10.

39 *The Leadership Imperative*, 32.

40 Ibid., 20.

41 Paul, *Leadership under Fire*, 40.

42 Robert Birnbaum, *How Academic Leadership Works: Understanding Success and Failure in the College Presidency* (San Francisco: Jossey-Bass), 73.

43 Bok, *Universities in the Marketplace*, 104.

44 Ibid.

45 University of Saskatchewan Act, 1995, s–73.

46 Chapter 6, p. 103.

Afterword: On the Global Talent Race

1 Ben Wildavsky, *The Great Brain Race: How Global Universities Are Reshaping the World* (Princeton: Princeton University Press, 2010).

2 Ibid., 4, 5.

3 See chapter 1.

4 Richard Florida, *The Rise of the Creative Class* (New York: Basic Books, 2002).

5 Turpin, *Canadian University Presidents Project*; and Paul, *Leadership under Fire*.

Select Bibliography

Altbach, Philip, Robert Berdahl, and Patricia Gumport. 1999. *American Higher Education in the Twenty-First Century: Social, Political, and Economic Challenge.* Baltimore: Johns Hopkins University Press.

Atkinson-Grosjean, Janet. 2006. *Public Science Private Interests, Culture and Commerce in Canada's Networks of Centres of Excellence.* Toronto: University of Toronto Press.

Axelrod, P.D. 2002. *Values in Conflict: The University, the Marketplace and the Trials of Liberal Education.* Montreal and Kingston: McGill-Queen's University Press.

Barnes, Patrick. 2007. *Economic Perspectives on Innovation and Invention.* Hauppauge, NY: Nova Science Publishers.

Bhidé, Amar. 2008. *The Venturesome Economy: How Innovation Sustains Prosperity in a More Connected World.* Princeton: Princeton University Press.

Bok, Derek. 2003. *Universities in the Marketplace.* Princeton: Princeton University Press.

Bolman, Lee, and Joan Gallos. 2011. *Reframing Academic Leadership.* San Francisco: Jossey-Bass.

Bowen, William. 2010. *Lessons Learned: Reflections of a University President.* Princeton: Princeton University Press.

Bradley, Richard. 2005. *Harvard Rules: The Struggle for the Soul of the World's Most Powerful University.* New York: Harper Collins.

Christensen, Clayton, Scott Anthony, and Erik Roth. 2004. *Seeing What's Next: Using the Theories of Innovation to Predict Industry Change.* Boston: Harvard Business School Publishing Corporation.

Christensen, Clayton, and Henry Eyring. 2011. *The Innovative University: Changing the DNA of Higher Education from the Inside Out.* New York: John Wiley and Sons.

Clark, Howard. 2003. *Growth and Governance of Canadian Universities: An Insider's View*. Vancouver: UBC Press.

Clark, Ian, Greg Moran, Michael Skolnik, and David Trick. 2009. *Academic Transformation: The Forces Reshaping Higher Education in Ontario*. Montreal and Kingston: Queen's School of Policy Studies, McGill-Queen's University Press.

Coates, Ken, and Carin Holroyd. 2007. *Innovation Nation: Science and Technology in 21st-Century Japan*. Basingstoke: Palgrave Macmillan.

Coates, Ken, and Bill Morrison. 2011. *Campus Confidential: 100 Startling Things You Need to Know about Canadian Universities*. Toronto: Lorimer.

Council of Canadian Academies. 2013. *The State of Industrial R&D in Canada*. Ottawa: The Expert Panel on Industrial R&D in Canada.

Doern, Bruce, and Jeffrey Kinder. 2007. *Strategic Science in the Public Interest, Canada's Government Laboratories and Science-Based Agencies*. Toronto: University of Toronto Press.

Etzkowitz, Henry. 2008. *The Triple Helix: Industry, University, and Government in Innovation*. London: Taylor and Francis. http://dx.doi.org/10.4324/9780203929605.

Fallis, George. 2007. *Multiversities, Ideas, and Democracy*. Toronto: University of Toronto Press.

Gambardella, Alfonso, and Franco Malerba, eds. 1999. *The Organization of Economic Innovation in Europe*. Cambridge: Cambridge University Press.

Johnson, Steven. 2010. *Where Good Ideas Come From: The Natural History of Innovation*. New York: Penguin.

Kao, John. 2007. *Innovation Nation: How America Is Losing Its Innovation Edge, Why It Matters, and What We Can Do to Get It Back*. New York: Free Press.

Kennedy, Donald. 1997. *Academic Duty*. Cambridge, MA: Harvard University Press.

Laidler, David, ed. 2002. *Renovating the Ivory Tower: Canadian Universities and the Knowledge Economy*. Toronto: C.D. Howe Institute.

Levin, Ben. 2005. *Governing Education*. Toronto: University of Toronto Press.

Manzer, Ronald. 2003. *Educational Regimes and Anglo-American Democracy*. Toronto: University of Toronto Press.

Ness, Roberta. 2012. *Innovation Generation: How to Produce Creative and Useful Scientific Ideas*. New York: Oxford University Press.

O'Mullane, Michael. 2011. *University Leadership: Approaches, Formation and Challenges in Europe*. Basingstoke: Palgrave Macmillan. http://dx.doi.org/10.1057/9780230346567.

Paul, Ross. 2011. *Leadership under Fire: The Challenging Role of a Canadian University President*. Montreal and Kingston: McGill-Queen's University Press.

Pierce, Susan. 2011. *On Being Presidential: A Guide for College and University Leaders*. Toronto: Jossey-Bass Higher and Adult Education.

Slaughter, Sheila, and Larry Leslie. 1997. *Academic Capitalism: Politics, Policies and the Entrepreneurial University*. Baltimore: Johns Hopkins University Press.

Thorp, Holden, and Buck Goldstein. 2010. *Engines of Innovation: The Entrepreneurial University in the Twenty-First Century*. Chapel Hill: University of North Carolina Press.

Trachtenberg, Steven Joel, Gerald B. Kauvar, and E. Grady Bogue. 2013. *Presidencies Derailed: Why University Leaders Fail and How to Prevent It*. Baltimore: Johns Hopkins University Press.

Von Hippel, Eric. 2005. *Democratizing Innovation*. Cambridge, MA: MIT Press.

Index

British Columbia Court of Appeal, 102–3
British Columbia Labour Relations Board, 102–3
British Columbia University Act, 103
Brownlee, Wayne, 78, 127
Brzustowski, Tom, 125–8, 130
Buckingham, Robert, 151–2

C9 League, 8
Calgary, 36, 107, 217
Canada, 4, 5, 9–11, 16, 21, 23–5, 31, 39, 40, 42–5, 48–50, 58, 61, 63, 68, 70, 75–7, 80, 86, 92, 103, 111–16, 118–26, 128, 130, 132, 134, 137, 138, 140, 150, 153–5
Canada Excellence Research Chairs (CERC), 16, 21, 36, 78
Canada Foundation for Innovation, 16, 121, 122, 124
Canada Graduate Scholarships, 25
Canada Institute for Health Research (CIHR), 16, 18, 27, 122–3, 164, 166
Canada Research Chairs, 16
Canadian Association of University Teachers (CAUT), 81, 83–9, 100, 106–7, 109, 135, 157, 172–3
Canadian Centre for Philanthropy, 70
Canadian Genetic Diseases Network (CGDN), 117
Canadian Light Source Inc. (CLS), 21, 111–12, 120–3
Canadian Press, 81
Canadian university senates study, 158
Cardinal, Douglas, 24
Carleton University, 80–2, 133
Centre for International Governance Innovation (CIGI), 83, 84, 86, 172

Chad, Karen, 20
Chakma, Amit, 24; Chakma Report, 24, 155
Charest, Jean, 43, 44
China, 27, 115, 153, 164
Clark et al., 57, 59, 169
Clayton H. Riddell Graduate Program in Political Management (GPPM), 80–2
collective bargaining, 91, 98–101, 106–9, 146, 158
Competition Review Panel, 10, 116
Conference Board of Canada, 10, 115
conférence des recteurs et des principaux des universités du Québec, 66
Conservative Party of Canada, 16
Conservative Party of Saskatchewan, 12
Continuing Education, Saskatchewan Department of, 13
corporate sponsorships, 73, 75; corporate donors, 78
corporatization, 5, 134, 135
Council of Canadian Academies, 10, 112, 115, 118–19, 125; Scientific Advisory Committee, 125
Council of Ontario Universities, 66
Crown Investments Corporation, 128

Dahl, Robert, 65
Dalhousie University, 11, 25, 142, 161
Danforth Plant Science Center, 79
Davenport, Paul, 133, 136
Desjardins, Martine, 45
DesRosiers, Edward, 14, 15; DesRosiers Report, 13–15, 17
Downey, Jim, 133
Downey, Keith, 129, 179
Doyle, Bill, 77

101, 103–5, 149; tenure, 34, 96,
101–7, 132, 148–51, 159
public policy, 4, 5, 16, 17, 25, 38, 51,
54, 55, 58, 60, 61, 70, 118–19, 144,
150, 154

QS World University Rankings, 8, 161
Quartier De L'Innovation, 129
Quebec, 41, 43–5, 58, 59
Queen's Park, 41
Queen's University, 133, 161, 164
Question Period, 71

Rae, Bob, 41, 166; Rae Report, 42, 43, 48
Regina, 19, 21, 70
Reindeer Lake, 77
Research and Innovation Council,
59, 118
research performance, 6, 9
Research Universities Council of
British Columbia, 66
Richardson, Doug, 174
Riddell, Clayton, 80
Riddell Family Charitable
Foundation (RFCF), 80, 81
Romanow, Roy, 14–15
Runte, Roseann, 133

Saskatchewan, 11, 15, 17–18,
20–3, 41, 43, 56, 59, 77, 79, 103, 107,
128–9, 141, 163, 179
Saskatchewan Court of Queen's
Bench, 104
Saskatchewan Department of Post-
Secondary Education, 14, 15
Saskatchewan Federation of Labour
(SFL), 98
Saskatchewan Indian Federated
College (SIFC). See First Nations
University of Canada

Saskatchewan Opportunities
Corporation, 128
Saskatchewan Party, 167
Saskatchewan Universities
Commission, 13–14, 163
Saskatoon, 15–17, 22, 23, 128–9, 163, 179
Saskatoon Cabinet Office, 14
Saskatoon Health Region, 18
Science, Technology and Innovation
Council of Canada, 10, 112, 115,
118, 162, 174; State of the Nation
Report 2008 and 2010, 112, 114
Scientific Research and Experimental
Development (SR&ED), 118
Scott, Walter, 11, 162
Shanghai Index, 9
Simpson, Jeffrey, 132
Skopik, Dennis, 111, 174
Smith, Stuart, 57
SNOLAB, 121, 123
Social Sciences and Humanities
Research Council (SSHRC), 123
Stager, David, 38–40
Statistics Canada, 422
St Aubyn, Edward, 9
Sudbury, 121
Supreme Court of British Columbia,
102
Supreme Court of Canada, 102
Sweden, 115

tenure. See promotion and tenure
Thiessen, Gordon, 94
Thomlinson, Bill, 122
Toronto, 13, 59, 129
Trachtenberg, Steven, 137
Trent University, 133
Triumf, 121
tuition, 5, 38–50, 54, 58, 124, 155–7,
166–8

Tuition Fee Policy Options for
Ontario, 42, 166
Turpin, David, 121, 132, 179

U15 group of universities, 8, 25–6,
67, 124
United Kingdom, 49, 115, 124, 161,
164
United States, 31, 70, 73, 75, 115, 124,
137, 138, 140, 146; Department of
Agriculture, 79
University of Alberta, 99, 142, 161,
164; Association of Academic
Staff, 99
University of British Columbia
(UBC), 68, 99, 101–3, 107, 133, 161,
164; UBC Faculty Association, 99,
103
University of Calgary, 25, 142, 161
University of Guelph, 142
University of Manitoba, 25, 142, 161
University of New Brunswick
(UNB), 133
University of Ottawa, 25, 125, 129,
161; Telfer School of Management,
125
University of Quebec, 45, 59
University of Regina, 12–15, 23, 59
University of Saskatchewan (U
of S), 3, 5–7, 11–17, 19, 20, 21,
23, 25, 27, 29, 30–3, 35, 37, 53,
78–9, 93, 103, 106–7, 111, 112,
120–2, 128–9, 141–2, 149, 151–2,
161–5, 167, 173; "Breakfasts at the
Club," 6; College Building, 11,
163; College of Agriculture and
Bioresources, 3, 21, 128; College
of Commerce/Edwards School

of Business, 98; College of Law,
27; College of Medicine, 18, 21;
Crop Development Centre, 21,
79; Department of Geology, 21;
Faculty Association, 98, 103,
104–5, 165; Faculty Club, 6; Issues
and Options, 30, 31; Provost's
Committee on Integrated
Planning, 33; Provost's White
Paper on Integrated Planning,
32; School of Environment
and Sustainability, 21; School
of Public Health, 21, 151–2;
strategic directions, 19, 30, 32, 34;
University of Saskatchewan Act,
104–5, 149; Western College of
Veterinary Medicine, 21, 69
University of Toronto, 75, 92, 99, 124,
133; Faculty Association, 99
University of Victoria, 121, 132
University of Waterloo, 83–6, 125,
129, 133
University of Wisconsin, 11
U of S. See University of
Saskatchewan
Usher, Alex, 42

Vancouver, 101, 121, 129
Vanier Canada Graduate
Scholarships, 16

Wall, Premier Brad, 77, 167
Washburn, Jennifer, 74, 75
Western University, 24, 142, 153
Wheater, Howard, 21
Wildavsky, Ben, 153–5
Wilfrid Laurier University, 83–6
World University Rankings, 8, 161